Measurement, Technology, and Individuality in Education

PROCEEDINGS OF THE 1982
ETS INVITATIONAL CONFERENCE

Ruth B. Ekstrom, *Editor*

NEW DIRECTIONS FOR TESTING AND MEASUREMENT
MICHAEL KEAN, *Editor-in-Chief*

Number 17, March 1983

Paperback sourcebooks in
The Jossey-Bass Social and Behavioral Sciences Series

Jossey-Bass Inc., Publishers
San Francisco • Washington • London

Ruth B. Ekstrom (Ed.)
Measurement, Technology, and Individuality in Education.
New Directions for Testing and Measurement, no. 17.
San Francisco: Jossey-Bass, 1983.

New Directions for Testing and Measurement Series
Michael Kean, *Editor-in-Chief*

New Directions for Testing and Measurement is published
quarterly by Jossey-Bass Inc., Publishers. Subscriptions, single-issue
orders, change of address notices, undelivered copies, and other
correspondence should be sent to *New Directions* Subscriptions,
Jossey-Bass Inc., Publishers, 433 California Street, San Francisco,
California 94104.

Editorial correspondence should be sent to the Editor-in-Chief,
Michael Kean, ETS, Evanston, Illinois 60201.

Library of Congress Catalogue Card Number LC 82-84211
International Standard Serial Number ISSN 0271-0609
International Standard Book Number ISBN 87589-901-3

Cover art by Willi Baum
Manufactured in the United States of America

Ordering Information

The paperback sourcebooks listed below are published quarterly and can be ordered either by subscription or as single copies. Subscriptions cost $35.00 per year for institutions, agencies, and libraries. Individuals can subscribe at the special rate of $21.00 per year *if payment is by personal check.* (Note that the full rate of $35.00 applies if payment is by institutional check, even if the subscription is designated for an individual.) Standing orders are accepted.

Single copies are available at $7.95 when payment accompanies order, and *all single-copy orders under $25.00 must include payment.* (California, Washington, D.C., New Jersey, and New York residents please include appropriate sales tax.) For billed orders, cost per copy is $7.95 plus postage and handling. (Prices subject to change without notice.)

To ensure correct and prompt delivery, all orders must give either the *name of an individual* or an *official purchase order number.* Please submit your order as follows:

Subscriptions: specify series and subscription year.
Single Copies: specify sourcebook code and issue number (such as, TM8).

Mail orders for United States and Possessions, Latin America, Canada, Japan, Australia, and New Zealand to:
Jossey-Bass Inc., Publishers
433 California Street
San Francisco, California 94104

Mail orders for all other parts of the world to:
Jossey-Bass Limited
28 Banner Street
London EC1Y 8QE

New Directions for Testing and Measurement Series
Michael Kean, *Editor-in-Chief*

Contents

Ruth B. Ekstrom

Because much of prior learning is incidental, rather than intentional, special measurement techniques are needed to demonstrate prior learning's relevance to existing educational and employment standards.

Introduction

The theme of this year's Invitational Conference, Measurement, Technology, and Individuality in Education, was chosen to promote better understanding of the effect that measurement and the computer have on education. Measurement and the computer do not have to require the learner to conform; rather they can allow us to adapt the educational process to the needs of each individual.

This year's conference was divided around two main foci: advances in measurement through technology, addressed in the papers by Green, Johnson, and Popham; and new approaches to measurement, addressed in the papers by Howard, Willingham, Tate, and Ekstrom.

Computerized adaptive testing allows us to create a unique personalized test for each individual. Growing out of item response theory and utilizing computer technology, this new approach allows each test to be tailored to match the ability and knowledge of the learner. As Bert Green tells us in Chapter One, computerized adaptive testing has other advantages, including allowing individuals to work at their own pace instead of within time limits, and allowing for a variety of new item types where individuals construct their own response instead of selecting from a few options.

The computer is only one of several technological tools that will help us measure things that we could not measure before. In Chapter Two, James Johnson describes new technologies, involving microelectronics, communications, and information science, that are being used to simplify and mechanize traditional measurement techniques. The next step will be to do things that were impossible before, using technologies like the video disc or the reading machine to analyze information analytically and intuitively.

These new technology-based measurement activities will change instruction as well as testing. One major change will be in achievement testing. In the past, the content of standardized achievement tests had to be general enough to satisfy the needs of diverse curricula. Changing needs, such as the need for improved public accountability, led to competency testing. Educators, in turn, began targeting instruction toward the competencies these tests measured. James Popham thinks that this situation provides test-makers with the opportunity to have a major impact on the curriculum. In Chapter Three, he suggests several strategies for measurement-based instructional improvement.

Achievement tests are familiar to everyone, but new approaches to measurement, like the assessment center, involve a wide variety of other testing techniques. In Chapter Four, Ann Howard describes how the Bell System has used this method to select managers. Using interviews, simulations, and projective tests, as well as paper-and-pencil tests, allows for an analysis of both motivation and abilities. Being able to assess what people do, not just what they say they do, makes better manager selection possible.

College admissions is another area in which it is often necessary to assess qualifications other than academic ability. Warren Willingham, in Chapter Five, describes the role personal achievements, goals and interests, and background characteristics play in college admissions and college success. As he points out, the broadened view of applicants from the assessment of personal qualities "helps to serve better the individuality of students, the multiple purposes of education, and the diverse needs of society."

One part of assessing personal qualities often involves asking students to evaluate their own experience and accomplishments. In this, the evaluation of personal qualities is similar to other situations requiring the evaluation of experiential learning. In Chapter Six, Pamela Tate outlines the major theoretical and practical problems in assessing both sponsored and prior experiential learning. Tate argues that the assessment issues for both types of experiential learning are the same and the perceived differences in these two types of learning are due to politics, history, and the characteristic of the learners.

In contrast, Ruth Ekstrom, in Chapter Seven, argues that prior experience learning often requires new and different kinds of measurement techniques. The most important difference between traditional learning and prior experience learning, she says, is whether the acquisition of knowledge was intentional or incidental. She describes methods that have been developed to identify and assess the prior experiential learning of adult women from their unpaid work in the home and the community.

These new measurement methods and technologies promise that, in the future, testing will be a more exciting intellectual challenge both for the test-takers and for the test-makers.

Gregory R. Anrig

Gregory R. Anrig is president of ETS.

The citation for the 1982 ETS Award for Distinguished Service
to Measurement summarizes Professor Cattell's contributions.

Citation: Raymond B. Cattell

In a remarkable career spanning over half a century, Raymond B. Cattell has made a prodigious number of landmark contributions to empirical knowledge and theory in psychology. He has persistently underscored the fundamental importance of wedding substance and method in a unified approach to measurement and empirical research. A continuing testament to this vision is the Society of Multivariate Experimental Psychology which he helped to found.

Although one might attempt to epitomize Professor Cattell's enormously productive career by listing his major contributions, such an account would lose sight of his singular and truly monumental accomplishment. This is a theory of human development that integrates the intellective, temperamental, and dynamic domains of personality in the context of environmental and cultural influences. This is not to ignore the importance of his many other contributions, such as his factor analytic mapping of functional unities of intelligence and personality, his delineation of the three basic media of assessment, his formalization of ipsative as differentiated from normative measurement, his insightful separation of fluid and crystallized intelligence and subsequent elaboration of the comprehensive triadic theory of intellect, and his numerous developments in the theory and technique of factor analysis, reliability, and validity. Although this impressive list may be extended literally for pages, its essence is that Raymond B. Cattell stands without peer in his quantitative integration of process and structure into a unified theory of learning, personality, and psychological measurement. In accomplishing this scholarly feat, Professor Cattell became a recognized expert in several substantive and methodological specialties simultaneously. Thus, he provides a model of the complete psychologist in an age of specialization.

For his many contributions to the theory and technique of psychological measurement and its practical applications in educational and clinical settings, and for his advancement of our understanding of intellective and personality structure and development, ETS is pleased to present its 1982 Award for Distinguished Service to Measurement to Raymond Bernard Cattell.

Previous Recipients of the ETS Measurement Award

1970 E. F. Lindquist

1971 Lee J. Cronbach

1972 Robert L. Thorndike

1973 Oscar K. Buros

1974 J. P. Guilford

1975 Harold Gulliksen

1976 Ralph Winfred Tyler

1977 Anne Anastasi

1978 John C. Flanagan

1979 Robert L. Ebel

1980 John B. Carroll

1981 Ledyard R Tucker

A computer can administer tests that are individually adapted to the ability of the test-taker.

Adaptive Testing by Computer

Bert F. Green

The computer revolution is upon us. There are computers in our cars, in the checkout stands at the market, in our living rooms. For years, computers have also been involved in testing; in keeping track of test form shipments, in scoring answer sheets, and in producing score reports. This chapter examines the advantages that come from having computers actually administer the tests.

Standardized tests work pretty well now, so the motivation for change is slight. Tests such as the College Board's Scholastic Aptitude Test (SAT) are highly reliable and often quite valid. When used for the purposes for which they have been designed, standardized tests are extremely useful. The SAT, for example, can help to identify those college applicants most likely to succeed academically at a particular college. The tests work much better than many test critics believe.

However, there is plenty of room for improvement. The field of standardized ability testing has been relatively static for decades. The tests of the 1980s are not much different from the tests of the 1950s. The usual paper-and-pencil format, with group administration, severely restricts what we are able to test. The computer can help us to get out of this straitjacket.

The past decade has seen vigorous developments of the methods of computerized adaptive testing (CAT). Lord (1970, 1971, 1977, 1980) and his colleagues at ETS have played a leading role in this development; as have Samejina (1969, 1977); Bock and Lieberman (1970); Urry (1977) and his col-

R. B. Ekstrom (Ed.). *Measurement, Technology, and Individuality in Education.* New Directions for Testing and Measurement, no. 17. San Francisco: Jossey-Bass, March 1983.

leagues at the Office of Personnel Management; Weiss (1974, 1978, 1979, 1980) and his group at the University of Minnesota; McBride (1980), Sympson (1982), and their colleagues at the Naval Personnel Research and Development Laboratory; and Ree (1981) at the Air Force Human Resources Laboratory.

Adaptive testing requires the application of the new test theory that Birnbaum (1968) discussed as latent trait theory, but that Lord now calls item response theory (IRT). Adaptive testing is one of the most important applications of IRT. Much of the impetus for the development of IRT and CAT came from the Office of Naval Research (ONR), under Farr, Davis, and others. They deserve great credit for supporting developments that have culminated in the current efforts to develop a CAT version of the Armed Services Vocational Aptitude Battery.

Testing by Computer

The computer achieves efficiency simply because it keeps testing on target. Nothing is more counterproductive than to confront a person of limited ability with a great many items that are too difficult, or to give a very able student a succession of easy items. Binet (1909) knew this when, at the beginning of this century, he devised the first standardized test of general academic readiness, which somehow got called intelligence. Binet reasoned that if someone answered a question correctly, a more difficult question was appropriate, but that when the person failed to answer items of a certain level, there was no point presenting harder questions. This process is fine for one-on-one testing — one test-giver and one test-taker. It is also useful in the psychophysical laboratory, when a listener's hearing is tested by raising and lowering a tone's intensity until the listener's threshold has been bracketed.

When large numbers of persons have to be evaluated, group-administered paper-and-pencil tests provide better standardization and easier administration. Computers offer an alternative. Although we can seldom afford to provide one test-giver for each test-taker, each examinee can receive a personalized test presented by computer with items uniquely selected to suit her or him. Computer presentation has many other virtues. It permits new types of items and greatly expands the range of possibilities. This will be discussed further in the next chapter. The opportunities for new items are still more potential than real, but computerized adaptive testing is feasible and is already being done on a regular, if limited, basis.

This modern adaptive test requires a computer, but computerized testing is certainly possible without adaptive features. At the recent convention of the American Psychological Association, many exhibitors were hawking computer systems that could automatically give and score the Minnesota Multiphasic Personality Inventory (MMPI), and a panoply of other personality questionnaires and ability tests. These systems are aimed at the overworked clinician who needs relief from boredom, not to mention a handy tax writeoff.

In my own state of Maryland, the Motor Vehicles Administration routinely gives its written driver's license examination by computer. Applicants of all ages and all walks of life see the multiple choice items presented, one at a time, on a computer terminal's TV-like screen and make responses on a special-purpose keyboard. Although some of the old paper-and-pencil tests are kept around for emergency use, most applicants find the computer-presented test very satisfactory. The Motor Vehicle Administration has discovered that computerized testing is a great boon to test security. Formerly, they used four test forms. The local commercial driving schools had keys to all four forms. Now each applicant gets a random selection of items from a large pool and can thus be evaluated fairly. The computer also saves time because it can impose a time limit. Since this is strictly a mastery test, the computer can also stop testing as soon as the test-taker falls below criterion, which in their case means four errors.

These examples indicate that computer-administered testing is a practical reality. But none of these systems is adaptive, in the sense of selecting the items most appropriate to the test-taker. That too is practical, but is a bit more complicated technically. Let us examine what is needed and how the procedure works.

Adaptive Testing Procedures

Consider a test of word knowledge, or vocabulary. First we need a large pool of items that have been carefully scaled for difficulty by pretesting. Further, those items should be discriminating. An item that is of moderate difficulty for persons who score 500 on the SAT scale should be very easy for persons who score 700, and quite difficult for persons who score 400. We will also need items that are of moderate difficulty for persons at the 300-score level, and other items that are moderately difficult for students in the 700-score range. In short, we need a broader spectrum of item difficulties than is customary on a conventional test.

When a candidate is ready to be tested, the computer starts by presenting an item that is of medium difficulty for the average student, which these days means a score of a bit above 400. Suppose the response of this particular student is correct. The computer then selects a considerably harder item — say a 500-level item. Suppose the student is correct again. A 600-level item will be given. If the student fails this item, the computer backs off, selecting an item scaled at about 550. An incorrect response will result in a still easier item; a correct answer leads to a more difficult item. After every item, the computer estimates the candidate's test score, based on the information so far, and selects as the next item one that will give the most additional information about the candidate's score.

Both the scoring and the item selection are done following procedures based on the new test theory called item response theory (IRT). The details of this test theory can be found in Lord's (1980) book, *Applications of Item Response Theory to Practical Testing Problems*. There are two or three slightly different procedures, all with the same general characteristics. Lord espouses the maximum likelihood procedures. Urry (1977) prefers a Bayesian procedure, whereas Bock and Aiken (1981) like a hybrid. In all cases, the calculations are formidable and a computer is needed. One might wonder if a computer can do the computation fast enough not to delay the next item. The computer avoids this necessity by making two alternative calculations while the current item is being presented. As the examinee is deciding which answer to select, the computer prepares for the two possible outcomes— a correct answer or an incorrect answer. The computer computes the score and selects the next item for either alternative; these are ready as soon as the response is made.

An especially valuable feature of item response theory is the central role played by test information. The reciprocal of test information is the variance of measurement errors, so the reciprocal square root of information is the standard error of measurement. Educational Testing Service (ETS) and other testing organizations have always tried to convince clients that the standard error of measurement was more important than reliability, but because reliability is needed in classical test theory in order to obtain the standard error of measurement, reliability has generally been the preferred index. In item response theory, reliability is a contrived index (Sympson, Weiss, and Ree, 1982). The natural index is the standard error of measurement or its blood relative, test information.

Moreover, test information is naturally a function of ability. Classical theory makes no provision for measurement error varying with score—only a single average value is given. A few persons, such as Mollenkopf (1949), have attempted to assess error as a function of ability. We know intuitively that a traditional test measures better in the middle and relatively poorly at the extremes. Item response theory quantifies this intuition explicitly.

Adaptive testing provides a means of controlling test information directly. At each stage in the process, the computer estimates the candidate's ability score and computes the total amount of information available about the score. The neatest stopping procedure is to stop when the standard error reaches a fixed, acceptably low level, which is to say when enough information has been obtained. In practice, a limit may be placed on the number of items presented, to guard against erratic response patterns. The net result is that, apart from the effects of such a limit, every score has the same standard error of measurement. If equal accuracy is not desired, the adaptive test can be modified to provide any specified error level for any score value. Those not familiar with the item response theory literature may wonder how a score is derived in an adaptive test. Adaptive tests use a maximum likelihood score based on scaled values of the items. In effect, the score is like a weighted average of the difficulties of the items answered correctly and the items answered incorrectly. The weights are complicated, depending on the discriminability of the item and, to a small extent, on the distribution of item difficulties.

Viewed from the perspective of the adaptive process, the conventional test's inefficiency is evident — no matter which examinee is considered, some of the items will be very inappropriate and many of the items will not be as appropriate as they might be. It is difficult to compare an adaptive test with a conventional test, because the error levels are different. A theoretical comparison can be made if one assumes either that the conventional test has a very broad range, or that the stopping rule of the adaptive test has been set to reproduce the error structure of the conventional test. In either case, it can be shown that the adaptive test needs only about half the number of items as the conventional test for equivalent results. Theoretical results have been reported by Green (1983) and others; empirical results have been reported by Weiss (1979), McBride (1980), and others. Since information per item in an adaptive test is twice the information per item in a conventional test, the adaptive test represents a 100 percent increment in information per item.

Some Problems

Have we lost anything in the adaptive process? We have lost whatever it is that a test editor does. The individual items have been well edited and highly selected, but the test is put together by the computer. One aspect that may need attention is balance in item content. If the items are truly one-dimensional this scarcely matters, but if the items have several secondary facets, some additional control is in order.

In constructing a conventional test, a test editor examines the complete test to see if the contexts of the items are reasonably balanced. Vocabulary items should not all be related to music, or to agriculture, or to city life. Because they must be related to something, their contexts should be varied and balanced. The contexts are not themselves at issue: Two cows plus five cows are seven cows, just as two taxis plus five taxis are seven taxis, but some students may be more at ease with taxis than with cows. To the extent that these context effects are deemed important, they will have to be stated explicitly — each item will have to be categorized and the system will have to try, in a secondary way, to balance categories when selecting items. As noted earlier, the range of item difficulties must be greater than is now common. Adaptive tests thus place extra demands on item writers so that test construction can be taken over by the computer.

Item calibration is a more serious undertaking in an adaptive test. More data and more complex calculations are needed. The extra effort is worthwhile because, if calibration is done well, test equating is automatic. One equating headache emerges when an adaptive test must be equated with a paper-and-pencil test, as might be the case when a change from one system to the other is being made gradually. I am one of a group of psychometricians now examining this problem for the armed services, who are planning to introduce a computerized version of the Armed Services Vocational Aptitude Battery in what will be the first widespread use of adaptive testing.

Some concern has been expressed about the fairness of adaptive tests, where everyone takes a different test. Individualized tests can be considered to be randomly parallel tests, as has been discussed by Lord and Novick (1968). These are an extension of the present procedure using many different forms of a test like the SAT. Viewed in this way, the tests are all equivalent. There is nothing unfair about not giving poor students a chance to try the hard items, nor is it unfair not to give the high scorers a chance to fail the easy items. In a track meet, a high jumper who can clear a six-foot bar need not jump a five-foot bar; conversely, a jumper who cannot clear a six-foot bar does not get the chance to try a six-and-a-half–foot bar.

Some persons have expressed concern about the use of computer terminals. Experience indicates that this is not a problem. This is the computer generation. It is a rare teenager who has not played Pac-Man, Space Invaders, or one of the other computer games. Pinball machines seem to have gone the way of buggy whips.

Advantages

Some secondary advantages of computer testing should be mentioned. One of the most attractive administrative advantages is improved test security. Although computers are not larceny-proof, tests are more secure in a computer system than in a desk drawer. With computers, there are no more messy answer sheets, no more ambiguity about students' responses, and no chance that the student will mark the wrong item on the answer sheet. Moreover, the test can be scored immediately and a computer record is automatically available for item analysis.

Perhaps the most intriguing psychometric advantage of individualized tests is that an examinee can work at his or her own pace, which yields an ideal power test. Present testing programs have time limits chosen to balance the time that the very able student must sit and wait with the time it takes for slow students to finish most of the test. In a computerized adaptive test, each examinee stays busy. Each examinee is challenged but not discouraged, since with multiple choice questions the best choice of difficulty is such that each person gets about three out of five items correct. When sophisticated software is unavailable, items can be unobtrusively slipped into the sequence for pretests. Finally, if the item pool is big enough, the entire pool can be published without compromising the test.

The computer benefit that is most fun to contemplate is the many opportunities for new kinds of items. There is the very real possibility of constructed responses. Certainly, numerical answers to arithmetic problems can be typed; probably responses to word fluency tests can be typed. Memory can be tested by use of successive frames. Cooper (1982) is testing spatial visualization by alternating a perspective view of an object with the standard plan views. Videodisc technology has developed to the point where a short dynamic sequence, that is, a video clip, can be presented as the stem of an item. A fireman's exam or a policeman's exam could show a situation and ask about proper procedure. Today this is done by long paragraphs of written description, which puts a heavy verbal load on what should not be verbal tests. Tests of diagnostic skill or problem-solving skill can require the examinee to seek the information actively. The possibilities are vast.

These advantages will follow when tests are given by computer. This is now economically and technically feasible. Equipment costs are coming down. Still, computer testing is best suited to a situation in which a few persons are tested every day. This is appropriate for the armed services and is a natural for personnel offices. On the other hand, testing programs like the College Board will have to change their procedures completely before they can use the system. Such changes can and eventually will be made. Indeed, it may even turn out that paper-and-pencil testing will follow pinball machines, slide rules, and buggy whips on the road to oblivion.

References

Binet, A. *Les ideés modernes sur les enfants.* Paris: Ernest Flammarion, 1909.

Birnbaum, A. "Some Latent Trait Models and Their Uses in Inferring an Examinee's Ability." In F. M. Lord and M. K. Novick (Eds.), *Statistical Theories of Mental Test Scores.* Reading, Mass.: Addison-Wesley, 1968.

Bock, R. D., and Aiken, M. "Marginal Maximum Likelihood Estimation of Item Parameters: Application of an EM Algorithm." *Psychometrika,* 1981, *46,* 443–459.

Bock, R. D., and Lieberman, M. "Fitting a Response Model for n Dichotomously Scored Items." *Psychometrika,* 1970, *35,* 179–197.

Cooper, L. *Strategies and Spatial Skill.* Paper presented at the American Psychological Association meeting, September, 1982.

Green, B. F. "The Promise of Tailored Tests." In H. Wainer and S. A. Messick (Eds.), *Principles of Modern Psychological Measurement. A Festschrift in Honor of Frederic Lord.* Hillsdale, N.J.: Erlbaum, 1983.

Lord, F. M. "Some Test Theory for Tailored Testing." In W. Holtzman (Ed.), *Computer-Assisted Instruction, Testing, and Guidance.* New York: Harper & Row, 1970.

Lord, F. M. "Robbins-Monro Procedures for Tailored Testing." *Educational and Psychological Measurement,* 1971, *31,* 3–31.

Lord, F. M. "A Broad-Range Tailored Test of Verbal Ability." *Applied Psychological Measurement,* 1977, *1,* 95–100.

Lord, F. M. *Applications of Item Response Theory to Practical Testing Problems.* Hillsdale, N.J.: Erlbaum, 1980.

Lord, F. M., and Novick, M. R. *Statistical Theories of Mental Test Scores.* Reading, Mass.: Addison-Wesley, 1968.

McBride, J. R. "Adaptive Verbal Ability Testing in a Military Setting." In P. Weiss (Ed.), *Proceedings of the 1979 Computerized Adaptive Testing Conference.* Minneapolis: Department of Psychology, University of Minnesota, September, 1980.

Mollenkopf, W. G. "Variations of the Standard Error of Measurement." *Psychometrika,* 1949, *14,* 189–229.

Ree, M. J. "The Effects of Item Calibrations, Sample Size, and Item Pool Size on Adaptive Testing." *Applied Psychological Measurement,* 1981, *5* (19), 11–19.

Samejina, F. "Estimation of Latent Ability Using a Response Pattern of Graded Scores." *Psychometric Monograph Supplement,* 1969, 17, entire issue.

Samejina, F. "The Use of the Information Function in Tailored Testing." *Applied Psychological Measurement,* 1977, *1,* 233–247.

Sympson, J. B., Weiss, D. J., and Ree, M. *Predictive Validity of Conventional and Adaptive Tests in an Air Force Training Environment.* AF HRL-TR-81-40. Air Forces Human Resources Laboratory, Brooks Air Force Base, Tex., March, 1982.

Urry, V. W. "Tailored Testing: A Successful Application of Latent Trait Theory." *Journal of Educational Measurement,* 1977, *14,* 181–196.

Weiss, D. J. *Strategies of Adaptive Ability Measurement.* Psychometric Methods Program, research report 74-5. Minneapolis: Department of Psychology, University of Minnesota, 1974.

Weiss, D. J. *Efficiency of an Adaptive Inter-Subject Branching Strategy in the Measurement of Classroom Achievement.* Psychometric Methods Program, research report 79-6. Minneapolis: Department of Psychology, University of Minnesota, 1979.

Weiss, D. J. (Ed.). *Proceedings of the 1977 Computerized Adaptive Testing Conference.* Minneapolis: Department of Psychology, University of Minnesota, 1978.

Weiss, D. J. (Ed.). *Proceedings of the 1979 Computerized Adaptive Testing Conference.* Minneapolis: Department of Psychology, University of Minnesota, 1980.

Bert F. Green is professor of psychology at the Johns Hopkins University. He is an adviser to an armed services project on computerized adaptive testing.

New information technology may allow us to come full circle back to individualizing measurement. In doing so, it presents unique challenges and opportunities.

Things We Can Measure Through Technology That We Could Not Measure Before

James W. Johnson

This chapter's purpose is to stimulate thoughts about how the new information technology can enhance testing of individuals and to look at what technology makes feasible that was not feasible before. Looking only at feasibility, however, ignores the normal course of technology adoption. In its first stage, technology replaces manual or traditional methods, and activities are performed faster or more effectively; in the second stage, technology fosters new applications, and things are done that were never done before; in the third stage, technology transforms or changes life styles. We are just now emerging from the first stage in using information technology. This first step is a necessary prelude for stimulating ideas of new things that can be done.

Before giving some examples of the enhanced power of information technology, it is perhaps useful to define the term and review some characteristics of information technology.

The New Technology

Information technology represents both a set of instruments and a concept. The instruments are computers, satellites, and the like; the concept is

R. B. Ekstrom (Ed.). *Measurement, Technology, and Individuality in Education.* New Directions for Testing and Measurement, no. 17. San Francisco: Jossey-Bass, March 1983.

13

that information is a valuable resource, like energy. Computers provide selectivity, manipulation of information, and a crude sort of intelligence—the power to decide based on rules—while communications provide highways for moving electronic traffic from place to place. The importance of information, long recognized in education, is reflected in a reversed emphasis on research and knowledge as the basis of a nation's economic strength.

The new technology consists of three key elements: microelectronics, communications, and information science. Together they form a powerful technology of considerable importance, an importance amplified because the cost of the technology is falling and because the technology brings together previously unrelated fields.

Microelectronics. Microelectronics, the basis of the new technology, reduces large, complex electrical circuits to very small, energy-efficient, reliable devices. These circuits may do traditional tasks such as amplifying or filtering out signals, but increasingly they carry out logical operations on digital signals. Logical operations of the form "if this occurs, do that" give electronic devices intelligence to respond to changing conditions.

Progress in microelectronic design is measured by the ability to etch as many circuits as possible on one quarter of a square inch of material called a chip. Now tens of thousands of logical circuits or storage locations can be put on a single chip, at a per-unit cost that is no more than if only ten circuits were put on it.

Because of their small size, microelectronic computers appear everywhere. Today automobiles, televisions, and microwave ovens contain intelligent microelectronic circuits that control combustion, picture brightness, and cooking. Tomorrow microelectronic devices will appear in light-sensitive light bulbs, climate sensors, and medical alarms attached to clothing.

Communications. Communication, the movement of information, is crucial to the new technology. While less well documented than developments in microelectronics, communication is changing rapidly as well. Traditional methods of communication—face-to-face meetings or the exchange of written words—are being replaced by electronic media such as telephones, radio, television, facsimile, and computers. Advances in electronic communication involve digital coding of voice, video, and data messages, and microelectronic switching. The transmission medium is changing from copper wires and broadcast transmitters to fiber optics, coaxial cables, laser beams, and space satellites. Electronics and new modes of transmission create potentially large savings; consider that it takes about one thousandth the energy to manufacture optical fiber than an equivalent length of copper wire, with a corresponding savings in space requirements. Additional savings occur by transmitting electronic images rather than printing information on paper.

Information Science. Information science provides concepts that help harness microelectronic and communication power for performing useful tasks. Information science includes mysterious sounding areas such as artificial intelligence, cognitive psychology, information engineering, decision theory, and data structures as well as the more familiar areas of computer science, programming, and systems analysis. Information sciences have helped us to recognize patterns in fingerprints and faces, to design efficient programs for accessing large data banks such as census data, and to produce methods of generating human speech.

A fascinating aspect of efforts to improve information processing by machine is the exploration of how humans solve problems, recognize patterns, and acquire new information. Much of the knowledge now used to recognize voices and human faces and to build robots for production work was first developed for purely scientific explorations in solving word problems and playing chess.

Costs and Convergence. While microelectronics, communications, and information science form the basis of the new technology, its acceptance comes from dramatically increasing performance and decreasing price and from joining previously unrelated telecommunications (telephone), mass communications (radio, television, motion pictures), and information processing (computation, data processing) technologies. Cost reduction and convergence are occurring so rapidly that the whole concept of information technology is changing.

Experts agree that cost trends will continue for the next decade with computing costs falling about 30 percent per year and communication costs about 20 percent per year. While these appear to be modest rates, a 25 percent reduction per year will reduce costs to one eighteenth of their current rate in ten years. Almost any process that can be described and represented electronically will be relatively cheap in the future.

Almost all technologies dealing with information, from typewriters to television shows, are using similar techniques and hardware. The keys are computer intelligence and digital coding of information ranging from pictures to music.

In many ways, the new information technology converges in the home. The telephone system provides worldwide computer access from 500 million homes; television provides display for a similar number. In the United States, vendors expect to sell 1 million home computers next year and have 3 million installed by 1984. Together, the television for data display and graphics, the telephone system to communicate with other computers and remote data bases, and the personal computer to provide programming are raw materials for a powerful intellectual tool.

What is so new about the new technology? After all, telephones, radios, televisions, and telegraphs have been around for a long time.

It is the microelectronic-based digital computer that gives all the other devices the intelligence to tailor their performance to a set of instructions. This intelligence means that a technology can be individualized and interactive, qualities not possible earlier.

The term *mass,* as used in *mass media* and *mass production,* describes an older technology that produced standard products at standard places at standard times. The new technology is demassed; video disk and video text let you choose your own sources, news, and other information, and computing lets you do these things interactively in your own home.

The combination of intelligence, low cost, and small size has created a superior technology that promises to be one of the great dramas of the next decade.

Technology and Measurement

The new information technology provides powerful new tools for those interested in measurement. The ways that the capability of microelectronic and artificial intelligence can be used to individualize measurement and testing are merely suggested here in hopes of providing the spark for new ideas.

First Applications. The first uses of technology have been, as predicted, to mechanize traditional methods. Scoring and analyses such as discrimination measures have been automated. In doing this, there is a tendency to adapt methods to the technology. Tests are made easy to score and analyses become more complex. For example, mark-sense answer sheets are used, and a factor of a cluster analysis becomes feasible with programs to do the computations.

At the next level, technology begins to be used to do things that were difficult or impossible to do with traditional methods. The best example is use of the branching—or "if, then"—capability of digital computers to provide adaptive testing. Test items can be sequenced, based on previous responses, to measure things more quickly and perhaps more deeply than before. In some ways, this replicates individual oral tests. In addition to the sequencing possible with interactive testing, response times can also be accumulated, adding another dimension to measurement. In general, the technology at this level offers the ability to individualize testing and measurement by using interactive methods provided by computers.

The capabilities I have described are possible with modest levels of computing, simple key entry, textual displays, and fairly restricted response processing. Several information technologies now appearing create possibilities far beyond what exists. They stretch the imagination.

Enhanced Technologies. New devices and techniques becoming available offer fantastic potential for presenting stimuli, capturing responses, and recognizing patterns. Consider the following currently available technologies.

A videodisc about the size of a long-playing record holds about thirty minutes of television. More significantly, it contains 54,000 separate frames, or screens, of information. Frames may be accessed by number and a series of frames can be played one at a time, at half speed, full speed, and so on. Under computer control, disk players can be programmed to respond to user actions. For example, a disk of art history slides may be combined with a computer-based indexing system to provide the appropriate slides based on artist, title, subject, time, and so on. A ballet quiz can present ten seconds of a step and ask the French or English name. In medicine, normal and pathological case slides can be presented and sequenced based on responses.

The possibilities for presenting nontextual or textual material are enormous, considering that a disc stores the equivalent of about five sets of the *Encyclopaedia Britannica.* Extended opportunities include pictorial conversations where students manipulate, sequence, and change images.

The Kurzweil reading machine can scan a page of typed or typeset text and convert it to voice output, reading out loud at varying speeds, repeating lines, and spelling words on request. The machine, when scanning text, has the capability of learning what shape character "c" is as opposed to "e," and can thus improve its skills. Once read, the text can be stored in a computer and played at a later time. Since the reader now only speaks according to American rules of pronunciation, it does poorly when reading German text. The text, however, can be read into a word processor, changed to American/English phonetics, and then spoken. Currently, the device is somewhat crude and expensive. Projections call for a pencil-sized scanner in a few years, at a cost of a few thousand dollars.

The Kurzweil reading machine is one example of using technology to aid those with disabilities — in this case, the blind. There are many whose abilities cannot be measured by normal methods who have new opportunities with technology.

Less exotic technologically, but perhaps as interesting as the Kurzweil reader, is the Writer's Workbench program developed at Bell Laboratories. The Writer's Workbench analyzes text and provides readability indices, word frequency counts, measures of use of the possessive case, and suggested rewrites.

Systems similar to the Writer's Workbench are now emerging from artificial intelligence centers to do tasks such as diagnosing machine malfunctions or identifying learning errors. Some of the most promising and elusive work involves interpreting natural language statements and matching them to existing knowledge bases. A commercially available system called Intellec translates English statements, such as "Tell me how many twelve-year-old children in Japan have parents who lived in the United States in 1970," into formal queries of data bases.

The use of some of these tools for measurement is in the preliminary stages, but the illustrations provide a glimpse of future possibilities.

Coming Full Circle

The first uses of technology probably served to restrict measurement to those things easily measured with mechanical devices. They have also encouraged, consistent with early technology forms, mass measurement and testing, locking in traditional methods. Contrast the use of a written instrument, with mark-sense responses analyzed by a computer program, with measurement conducted by an individual. The individual may use multiple senses, sight, smell, taste, sound, and touch and may analyze the information received in a variety of ways, analytically or intuitively. Both have their place.

The message of the new technology is that it can deal with sight, sound, and words as well as, in some cases, things not sensed by humans but measured by biological implants and the like. It can process ambiguous or natural language responses. And it does have the potential for including intuitive judgments as well as providing tools for greater insight by allowing easy manipulation of data.

Effective use of these tools will require a degree of understanding not needed in the past. For example, artificial intelligence techniques try to mimic human behavior. Standard methods only make mistakes when there are errors in their algorithms or data; their decision making is strictly logical. Artificial intelligence systems often depend on educated guesswork to reach conclusions — this extends to their ability to reach conclusions, but it can also lead to mistakes, even when data are correct.

While technology offers the opportunity to come full circle back to individualizing measurement and testing, it also offers new challenges. I hope we will be up to them.

James W. Johnson is director of the office of information technology at the University of Iowa. He has served as director of academic computing, director of CONDUIT, and associate professor of economics. During 1981 and 1982, he conducted a study of the impact of information technology on the university.

*Circumstances present today's measurement specialists with
an unparalleled opportunity to create achievement tests
that can enhance the quality of schooling.*

Measurement as an Instructional Catalyst

W. James Popham

Most of today's educational measurement specialists arrived at their present views regarding assessment by traveling a rather traditional testing trail. We learned about tests of various sorts when we were students in graduate classes or by reading the standard psychometric literature. For the most part, that literature consisted of textbooks written by established psychometric stars or of articles written by authors whose manuscripts had survived the traditional values of journal editors and referees.

Lest I misrepresent my own status in this recounting of how measurement folks arrived at their current conceptions of testing, I was as modal as could be. As had most of my contemporaries, I mastered a few traditional books about educational testing and subsequently attempted to keep up with the measurement literature by reading articles not too drenched with formulas.

My colleagues and I learned that achievement tests, particularly those that were nationally standardized, could be used to obtain an accurate estimate regarding how much students knew about a particular subject, such

I am indebted to Elanna S. Yalow for her excellent suggestions regarding an earlier version of this chapter.

R. B. Ekstrom (Ed.). *Measurement, Technology, and Individuality in Education.* New Directions for Testing and Measurement, no. 17. San Francisco: Jossey-Bass, March 1983.

as mathematics. We also discovered that aptitude and personality tests could often provide us with relatively accurate predictions about what would happen to examinees in the future. Making allowances for a less-than-perfect predictive precision of measurement, we recognized that various sorts of aptitude and personality tests could be most helpful to educators and counselors who wanted to make decisions about individuals. But, because I wish to restrict my remarks to large-scale achievement tests, I will say little more about aptitude or personality measures.

The Time-Honored Role of Educational Achievement Tests

Educational achievement tests may have been with us for centuries. Perhaps archeologists will someday unearth artifacts conclusively demonstrating that paleolithic professors gauged their students' mastery of hand-axe honing or dinosaur tracking with some sort of performance test. In the case of dinosaur tracking, this would constitute a binary-choice, or life-or-death, assessment technique.

Although this is exaggerated a trifle, it does seem that teacher-made achievement tests have been with us for eons. Commercially published achievement tests have been plentiful in the United States for even longer than I have been alive.

When most of us first learned about commercially published educational achievement tests, I think it is fair to say that we perceived some sort of relationship between those tests and instruction. After all, educational tests were supposed to yield an estimate of what an examinee had achieved, that is, learned. But it was a very general estimate, cast chiefly in relative terms. We thought it proper that standardized achievement tests accomplished their mission by comparing examinees with one another. After all, the chief use of standardized achievement tests in those days was to help educators identify students who were extremely knowledgeable, extremely unknowledgeable, or whose achievement test standings failed to mesh with their aptitude test standings.

Well before Glaser (1963) dubbed such examinations as "norm-referenced" tests, most of us were satisfied that large-scale standardized achievement tests merely yielded a pretty fair notion of what examinees knew. We thought that it was not only possible but also eminently sensible to compare examinees with one another on the basis of test score percentiles, according to the performance of a norm group. Few people working in educational testing in the 1940s and the 1950s voiced any dismay over the link between such tests and what went on in public schools.

Testing specialists who devoted themselves to the creation of large-scale achievement tests in those days were not driven by a responsibility to ensure that their measures actually influenced the nature of the instructional process. On the contrary, it was the mission of standardized achievement tests to reflect the effects of the educational system—not to shape it. Educators who taught to the test were thought to have committed instructional sins sufficient to send them to pedagogical purgatory. Large-scale achievement tests were supposed to mirror the nature of education, not mold it.

Achievement Test Impact

Given the conception of achievement testing prevalent during the 1950s and before, what were the effects of educational achievement test results on educational practice? Not surprisingly, such effects were minimal.

Although scores on large-scale measurement tests were sometimes aggregated, so that it was possible to see how a district or a state stacked up against national norms, in general only marked atypical results caused any stir in educational circles. We do, after all, live in a rather competitive society. Affluent school districts whose pupils outshone the rest of the nation on achievement tests took special pride in that accomplishment. School district officials whose pupils scored much lower than the rest of the nation became distressed with their students' low relative standings—although there are few recorded instances of such low-scoring districts thereafter turning matters around. Thus, for the most part, pupil performance on large-scale achievement tests had precious little impact on the actual nature of instruction.

Such test results were used by teachers to identify individual learners who needed special attention, particularly those underachievers whose achievement test scores were substantially lower than their aptitude test scores. In general, the use of large-scale achievement testing in this nation had little impact on the way education was conducted. Moreover, measurement specialists believed that this was as it should be. It was not the responsibility of testing people to tamper with the educational process. Such tampering was left in the tenacious hands of teachers and school administrators.

The primary reason that the results of districtwide and statewide achievement tests made little difference in educational practice is quite clear: There were no substantial contingencies riding on the results of those tests. Few people outside the educational community even knew what the results of large-scale testing programs were. In those days, the news media rarely gave any coverage to test results. Perhaps this was because test scores were rather high, and good news is no news. There were no major exposés of schools gone sour. The chief use of achievement test results was to help make instructional decisions, such as grouping students by their abilities. Up until the mid-1960s in America, educational achievement testing was a decisively low-stakes game.

Enter ESEA

All that changed in 1965, although few of us recognized it at the time. The passage of the Elementary and Secondary Education Act (ESEA) by the United States Congress in 1965 required that certain programs, funded under provisions of that legislation, be evaluated. Congressional lawmakers, skeptical of the virtues of large federal support for local education programs, set up requirements calling for the mustering of annual evidence regarding program quality.

At the outset, few educators really grasped what these new evaluation requirements entailed. For most of us, the term *evaluation* had more to do with grading students than with gauging the effectiveness of an educational endeavor. As if federal evaluation mandates were not enough, many state lawmakers followed suit. Much state-level funding for education programs in the late 1960s and the early 1970s was accompanied by a requirement to evaluate program quality.

In the early post–ESEA years, educators' efforts to evaluate their programs were marked more by floundering than by finesse. Yet, stumble by stumble, educators began to grasp that most of those policymakers who required educational evaluations were demanding at least one indispensable element in all evaluations: evidence of pupil growth. Almost without exception, that demand translated into test scores. Those who were dispensing dollars to improve education were calling for improved test scores. Legislators were not satisfied merely by assurances from program personnel that dollars were being well spent. Legislators wanted hard data showing that the taxpayers they represented were getting their money's worth.

Sensing this call for proof, educational program personnel set about to corral the test scores that would demonstrate to the world that their cherished educational interventions were indeed effective. Naturally enough, program evaluators in the late 1960s turned to the many standardized achievement tests available from commercial publishers. In general, these were carefully developed tests, accompanied by reams of solid psychometric data regarding reliability and validity. The normative data for these commercially published achievement tests were also impressive. To be sure, many of the commercially published norm-referenced tests of the late 1960s were first-rate assessment instruments.

The only problem with them was that, for purposes of program evaluation, they did not work. Program evaluators who relied on commercially published achievement tests to demonstrate program effects often demonstrated no effects at all. Abetted by hindsight, we can see that the nature of those achievement tests almost certainly doomed program evaluators to a string of "no significant difference" conclusions. For one thing, the tests were published by commercial firms that had to make the content of the tests general enough to satisfy a nation whose curricular predilections were diverse. As a result, there was often a substantial mismatch between what was emphasized on the test and what was emphasized in the program being evaluated. For another thing, many of the test items covering important curricular content had been excised from the tests because those items were answered correctly by too many examinees and therefore contributed insufficiently to producing the variation in scores so necessary to efficient norm-referenced measures. Often the very items that would have helped detect program improvement had already been jettisoned from commercially published standardized achievement tests.

For these and other reasons (Popham, 1981), program evaluators of the late 1960s and early 1970s began to lose confidence in the capability of standardized achievement tests to produce positive evidence regarding program quality. Even in settings where program personnel and program evaluators were certain that there was an effective program under way, scores on traditional standardized tests failed to demonstrate such effectiveness. In the absence of evidence that a program was effective, more than a few successful educational programs were cut loose by funding agencies.

"For the want of a nail, a shoe was lost. For the want of a shoe, a horse was lost. For the want of a horse, a general was lost. For the want of a general, the battle was lost. All for the want of a nail."

A similar epitaph could be inscribed on the tombstone of many successful but terminated educational programs of the 1960s and the 1970s. "All for the want of a test."

But the experiences of educational evaluators in that era brought home one powerful lesson to educators: Educational achievement tests could no longer be regarded as innocuous appendages to the educational enterprise. Those tests were being employed to make keep-or-kill decisions about education programs. Big dollars, sometimes millions of dollars, were riding on the results of achievement tests. More than ever before, the stakes associated with educational achievement tests had risen. The days of penny ante assessment were over.

Competency Testing Arrives

If the stakes associated with test results used for program evaluation had risen appreciably, those stakes soared with the advent of competency testing programs, particularly those that tied high school diplomas to student performance on a test. In the mid-1970s, a host of states enacted laws or regulations obliging high school students to pass competency tests, usually in the basic skills, before being granted a high school diploma. These assessment programs were enacted to placate an incredulous public that believed too many students were receiving high school diplomas on the basis of seat-time rather than mastery of basic skills. To counteract the perceived awarding of counterfeit diplomas, nearly forty states established some sort of competency testing program in which various contingencies were linked to the student's passing of the test.

In some states, for example, passing the test was a requirement for receiving a high school diploma. In other states, failure to pass such tests resulted in notification to the failing student's parents or to next year's teachers of those students. Elsewhere, failing students were identified so that they could receive remedial assistance in the basics. With few exceptions, a significant contingency hung on the student's test performance.

Public school educators are no fools. They realized quickly that, although students might be the apparent and immediate targets of competency testing programs, next in line could be the educators themselves. Few teachers relished the prospect of dealing with a disgruntled parent whose youngster had, after twelve years of ostensibly appropriate public schooling, been denied a diploma because of poor performance on a competency test. Even if a diploma were not at issue and the consequence of poor performance were merely remediation, few educators yearned for the opportunity to transmit a "your child needs renovation" message to parents.

Because the competency testing regulations called for the use of tests to have students demonstrate proficiency, could educators take a chance that the tests used would not give educators an opportunity to succeed? Setting legal implications aside for now, the answer is clear.

Once the competency testing movement shifted into high gear, it was evident to educators that, unless they wanted to deny diplomas to droves of students, competency tests must be selected on which students had a chance to succeed. Because, since the late 1960s, norm-referenced achievement tests had been pummeled as instructionally insensitive, most educators charged with implementing competency testing programs scurried toward criterion-referenced tests. In the absence of numerous commercially published criterion-referenced tests, educators at the state and district levels often constructed their own versions of criterion-referenced competency tests.

An appraisal of many of these homegrown competency tests suggests they were better suited for the paper shredder than for student assessment. If the road to hell is paved with good intentions, then the road to rotten competency tests is doubtless covered with the same sort of asphalt. In spite of lofty intentions by local educators, the bulk of these locally constructed competency tests were patently puerile. In addition to their pervasive psychometric shortcomings, most of them suffered from a fundamental flaw — they demanded too little of students.

In many instances, of course, these competency assessment enterprises were billed as "minimum competency testing programs." For some programs, it would have been more apt to label them as the "most minimum imaginable competency testing programs." I fear that the educators who whipped up many of these trivial assessment instruments were often doing so out of blatant self-interest. The more taxing the competency tests were, the more numerous the students who might fail them, and the more instructional failures that would be ascribed to educators. Few students would be challenged by cream-puff competency tests. Few educators who used such tests would encounter much static from parents.

In fairness to those educators who were trying to create decent competency testing programs, it is true that many teachers and administrators were struggling with problems for which they had scant preparation. To isolate defensible minimum skills sounds easier than it actually is. Some of these well-intentioned educators may have opted for undemanding competencies out of inexperience instead of self-interest.

At any rate, it is surely charitable to appraise the quality of competency tests created by school districts during the past half dozen years as variable. In my estimate, among the spate of competency tests sired in the 1970s, there were far more losers than winners. But, quality considerations aside, we learned a significant lesson during that period: namely, educational tests with important contingencies serve as powerful magnets for instruction.

Educators, sensing immediately that student success on competency tests was important, quickly aimed their instructional programs, at least in part, toward the competencies ensconced in those new tests. If a high school graduation test assessed a competency calling for students to demonstrate prowess in the use of such reference tools as the thesaurus, then it often took little time until that district's teachers were providing instructional units in the semantic subtleties of the thesaurus. The more clearly that the tests' competencies were explicated, the more targeted was the instructional effort to promote learner mastery of those competencies.

These teachers were not teaching to the test in the sense that they were coaching students to answer particular test items. Instead, the teachers were doing what sensible instructors ought to do: They were providing students with ample time on task, that is, practice relevant to the competency being taught. As never before in America, teachers saw that clear and important contingencies were associated with student performance on competency tests. Consequently, those tests served as powerful galvanizers of instruction. As never before in America, the nature of tests influenced the nature of teaching.

Instructional Validity and Constitutionality

As if pressures to avoid failure were not enough to force educators to rivet their attention on the content of competency tests, along came Debra P. *v.* Turlington, the legal contest regarding the legitimacy of Florida's high school graduation test. After a federal district court had ruled in July 1979 that Florida had the right to impose a competency test as a graduation requirement, the Fifth U.S. Circuit Court of Appeals decreed in May 1981 that no evidence had been present to demonstrate that Florida students had been given preparation to pass the test. The appellate court directed the state of Florida to assemble evidence that appropriate preparation had been provided to students by the state's schools. If no such preparation had been provided to students for the Florida graduation test, the Appeals court contended that its use to deny students diplomas was clearly unconstitutional on the grounds that such a test violated the equal protection and due process clauses of the U.S. Constitution.

The prospect that a district's or state's tests might be ruled unconstitutional on the grounds of insufficient preparation provided yet another spur for educators to focus their instruction on the competencies measured in their tests. To face the prospect of losing a court case was bad enough, but to lose a court case because one's test was unconstitutional! Such an event smacked of repudiating all things worthwhile in America's heritage. Having a test labeled unconstitutional was decisively worse, in most educator's estimates, than having a test labeled unreliable.

The more American educators heard about the Debra P. case and instructional validity, the more they strove to make their instructional programs mesh with any tests they were using to make key decisions about students. Again, tests served as instructional magnets—and this time those magnets carried U.S. Court of Appeals clout.

Reality Recognition: A Time of Opportunity

Whether or not measurement specialists like it, the assessment game has changed. Achievement tests are no longer ancillary afterthoughts to an ongoing instructional enterprise. On the contrary, those who control the nature of achievement tests now have the potential to exercise immense impact on the curriculum. We can either bemoan this new reality, hoping it will soon evaporate, or we can recognize our current assessment situation and take advantage of it. I prefer the latter option.

I think we should grasp the opportunity now available to us because I am convinced that the introduction of adroitly conceptualized educational achievement tests can constitute the most cost-effective scheme to enhance the quality of American education. Although augmenting the caliber of teachers or of textbooks is a more potent way of improving education, both of those improvement strategies carry hefty price tags. Boosting instructional quality by creating more potent testing targets can secure substantial improvement dividends for modest financial investment.

How, then, can we go about using the present set of circumstances to employ achievement tests as a springboard for improved instructional quality? I shall conclude this analysis with some suggestions regarding a measurement-based instructional improvement strategy.

A Manageable Number of Targets

We learned an important lesson in the heyday of behavioral objectives some years ago, namely, that highly specified instructional intents do not automatically yield instructional improvements. The hoped-for instructional improvements didn't arise, because educators were overwhelmed by interminable lists of miniscule behavioral objectives. Too many targets turned out to be no targets at all. Teachers simply could not attend to litanies of objectives, no matter how crisply those objectives were specified.

In much the same vein, we should make certain that the achievement tests we now hope will serve as instructional targets contain a reasonable number of assessment foci, so that teachers can organize their instructional efforts around a reasonable number of instructional foci. Instead of a competency test with fifty specific objectives, tests should be organized around a half-dozen or so competencies. These competencies should be stated at a level of generality, albeit still clear and measurable, which permits the competencies to subsume lesser, en route behaviors.

A number of states and school districts use competency tests in reading, for instance, with only five or six competencies. In mathematics, we find competency tests being used with only six or seven competencies. Similar competency tests have been created in other fields. With a manageable number of targets such as these, teachers can direct their energies to a set of targets that can be comprehended and monitored. Because these assessment targets can be conceptualized so that, though clear and measurable, they capture a rich array of subordinate skills, even a limited number of such targets can constitute a worthwhile aspiration.

There is, of course, the ever-present danger of curricular reductionism, that is, the tendency of teachers to teach only toward the competencies embedded in the test, thus overlooking other important content and competencies not measured by that test. If schools concentrate on only a modest number of competencies found in, for example, a high school graduate test, then students and society surely will have been shortchanged. But such a negative consequence need not occur. It need not be the case if the competencies embodied in the tests can be crafted so that instruction directed toward those targets can be more efficient. More effective instruction will leave ample time for the pursuit of other instructional emphases. Let's turn, therefore, to tests that illuminate instructional design, and therefore make instruction more effective.

Instructionally Illuminating Tests

When measurement specialists create tests that will serve as targets for instruction, they should create criterion-referenced tests. In the construction of criterion-referenced tests, the test developer is obliged to delimit the domain of examinee behavior being measured, including all eligible content. It is this domain of measurable behavior to which test scores will subsequently be referenced. It is the careful delineation of this domain of criterion behavior that constitutes the essence of a properly constructed criterion-referenced test.

But, and this point is pivotal, in almost all such test development efforts, those who circumscribe the domain of behavior being assessed have numerous options regarding how they delineate the behavior. Among the factors to be considered in those choices are the difficulty of the skill/content to be tested, the generalizability of the particular assessment strategy chosen to different assessment strategies, and the fidelity of the assessment scheme to the real-life demands for which the test presumably serves as a proxy indicator. Another factor to be considered when circumscribing the nature of the test is the extent to which the domain of tested behavior, as measured, illuminates instructional design decisions.

Without going into elaborate detail, for this point has been treated elsewhere (Popham, 1981), it is possible to deliberately conceptualize a domain of behavior to be tested on a criterion-referenced test so that the likely instructional requisites to promote student mastery of that behavior are incorporated into the assessment strategy itself. To illustrate, in a multiple-choice test there might be three criteria that must be embodied in each correct answer option. Each of these criteria could be isolated in the test's specifications. Each criterion could be formulated in the test specifications so that it could be readily understood by teachers and transmitted to learners. With regard to the test items' distractors, again each could embody a clearly understandable and teachable type of error. In sum, key elements in the test specifications could be fashioned so as to set forth crucial measurement factors in a manner conducive to instructional design. As long as tests can serve as magnets for instruction, why not make those magnets instructionally clarifying?

Choosing What Is to Be Assessed

As creators of criterion-referenced tests set forth their test specifications, that is, the rules that operationalize the test's items, they have enormous discretion in selecting the intended instructional targets. Teachability is clearly not the whole ballgame. It is often easier to teach the trivial than the profound.

Decisions regarding the things that tests should measure are receiving substantial scrutiny these days. In personnel testing, for example, the relevance of a test to the job for which it is being used as a screening device must be demonstrated (Uniform Guidelines of Employee Selection Procedures, 1978). Similarly, the courts have ruled that the content of tests must bear a clear relationship to the purpose to which the test's results will be put.

Thus, constructors of today's high-stakes tests no longer have the luxury of casually establishing a test blueprint with content categories on one axis and Bloom's cognitive levels on the other. The courts may well require a more formidable display of test-developer perspicacity in the determination of what is to be tested and, ultimately, taught.

At the very least, seeking the counsel of concerned clienteles seems to constitute an important first step in the delineation of that which is to be tested. If, for example, a basic skills test is to be employed as a device to verify that high school graduates can get along in a post-high school world, then the counsel of a wide variety of citizens should be sought regarding what sorts of skills are truly requisite in life. Decisions on such matters made exclusively by academicians are sure to be suspect. Why not let students in on the content-determination of tests? Students certainly have a substantial interest in such assessment endeavors.

Putting it more directly, because test scores are being used to make important decisions about pupils, and thus are influencing the nature of instructional practice, test-makers should be certain that all those who have a legitimate stake in these decisions have an opportunity to offer advice regarding what is to be measured.

An Alliance Between Testers and Teachers

Testing has become far too important to leave to the testers. Today's psychometric specialists can no longer remain blithely indifferent to what is going on in classrooms. Unlike the past, when we created after-the-fact assessment tools that often were only loosely tied to a given instructional program, we are now serving as educational pied pipers. Even if we don't want to, we currently command a formidable curricular following. This is a new and heavy responsibility. We can't escape that responsibility by pretending it doesn't exist.

In this context, today's testing specialists have only two professionally responsible options open to them. They can personally acquire the instructional skills for making tests aimed at praiseworthy targets, or they can establish collaborative alliances with those who possess the instructional acumen necessary for the development of tests that satisfy today's new instructional demands. Because few measurement specialists will be inclined to refurbish themselves with instructional skills, the latter option seems more likely to succeed.

By establishing collaborative relationships with instructionally astute colleagues, then when achievement tests are to be produced, testing specialists and their instructionally skilled cohorts will be able to create assessment instruments that can serve as beneficial catalysts for instruction. Teaching can be dramatically improved by testing.

Although circumstance, not our own doing, has allowed this fate to befall us, measurement specialists can seize this opportunity to enhance the quality of education. It is an opportunity that may come our way only once.

References

Glaser, R. "Instructional Technology and the Measurement of Learning Outcomes: Some Questions." *American Psychologist,* 1963, *18* (7), 519–521.

Popham, W. J. *Modern Educational Measurement.* Englewood Cliffs, N.J.: Prentice-Hall, 1981.

Uniform Guidelines on Employee Selection Procedures. *Federal Laws.* 401:2231-2277. Washington, D.C.: The Bureau of Internal Affairs, 1978.

W. James Popham is a professor in the graduate school of education at the University of California, Los Angeles. He is also director of the IOX, a Los Angeles-based test development agency. His most recent books are Criterion-Referenced Measurement *and* Modern Educational Measurement.

The complexity of managerial abilities and motivation is displayed in the assessment center method, where judgments depend on a comprehensive package of such techniques as paper-and-pencil tests, interviews, simulations, and projective tests.

Measuring Management Abilities and Motivation

Ann Howard

More than two decades ago, the Bell System pioneered in bringing to business, government, and educational organizations a robust method for measuring management abilities and motivation. Not even the developer of the technique, Dr. Douglas W. Bray at American Telephone and Telegraph (AT&T) realized in the mid-1950s that this method, called an assessment center, would spread into thousands of organizations by the 1980s. Each year it affects the lives of several hundred thousand persons who are evaluated in such centers, primarily to aid in promotion decisions. The background and philosophy of this method and its primary characteristics will be described in the pages that follow. Some illustrations of its use will be borrowed from two longitudinal, basic research studies of managers in the Bell System.

Background and Philosophy

The assessment center method is built on a philosophy of multiples, of two or three heads being better than one when it comes to making judgments about other's capabilities. The multiple notion applies not only to having more than one observer or assessor for each assessee, but also to the use of several different exercises to measure several different constructs or dimensions within the complex domain of managerial abilities and motivation.

R. B. Ekstrom (Ed.). *Measurement, Technology, and Individuality in Education.* New Directions for Testing and Measurement, no. 17. San Francisco: Jossey-Bass, March 1983.

The creative inspiration for this technique came from Dr. Henry Murray, who was engaged at the Harvard Psychological Clinic in the 1930s to study personality (Murray, 1938). A physician-turned psychological theorist, Murray proposed having various staff members at the clinic use their favorite techniques for studying personality on the same subjects. Evaluations of each subject were then compiled by having each researcher report his or her findings in a diagnostic council, modeled after the medical practice of having one expert testify about hospital patients' x-rays, another about blood work-ups and so forth.

Murray made the important addition of group and individual simulations to the assessment repertoire when he was invited by the Office of Strategic Services (OSS) to set up a center to select spies during World War II. A book documenting this OSS experience (Office of Strategic Services, 1948) was the inspiration for Bray's use of the assessment center to study the characteristics of managers. Bray had been hired at AT&T in early 1956 to begin a longitudinal study of how managers develop in a large organization. He launched the project, called the Management Progress Study, later that year, using the assessment center method merely as a research tool. Before the first summer's assessment was over, however, it became clear that the method could be used to identify those persons most likely to become the best managers. Within two years, Michigan Bell had begun the first operational use of the method for the actual selection of managers.

Assessment Center Components

There are several critical components for a method to be legitimately called an assessment center as we now know it.

Dimensions. The center is constructed and organized around a set of dimensions which represent the characteristics that are being measured. The search for dimensions begins with a proper job analysis, which defines the duties and responsibilities of the job for which applicants are being assessed. In practice, though, a fairly common set of complex but seemingly universally important dimensions is often employed, such as decision-making or leadership skills. The job analysis usually results in dimensions being added to or subtracted from this common core. Staff members focus on these dimensions during their observations of assessees' performance, for they will be required to rate each person's standing on each of these important characteristics, usually on a five-point scale, at the end of the assessment center process.

The original Bell System research used twenty-six different dimensions, although operational centers usually employ a more limited set. These dimensions were factor analyzed by the early researchers (Bray and Grant, 1966) to reveal seven clusters of dimensions that they felt were important in the overall rating of management potential.

1. Administrative Skills: The keys to success here are decision making measuring how ready a person is to make decisions and how good those decisions are; and organization and planning, or how effectively the person organizes his or her work plans ahead.

2. Interpersonal Skills: A high potential manager makes a forceful and likeable early impression on others—personal impact; has good oral communication skills; can lead a group to accomplish a task without arousing hostility—leadership skills; and can modify his or her behavior to reach a goal—behavior flexibility.

3. Intellectual Ability: General mental ability and a wide range of interests are important to success in this category. Tests of intelligence, scholastic aptitude, and learning ability measure the cognitive functions characterized as general mental ability.

4. Stability of Performance: A good potential manager maintains effective work performance under uncertain or unstructured conditions—tolerance of uncertainty—and in the face of personal stress—resistance to stress.

5. Work Involvement: Those rated high in managerial motivation find satisfactions from work more important than satisfactions from other areas of life—primacy of work—and want to do a good job even if a less good one is acceptable to the boss and others—inner work standards.

6. Advancement Motivation: Also indicative of high managerial motivation is the desire to be promoted significantly ahead of one's peers—need for advancement; a lack of concern for job security—low need for security; and an unwillingness to delay the reward of advancement too long—low ability to delay gratification.

7. Independence of Others: A high potential manager is not greatly concerned with gaining approval from superiors or peers—low need for superior approval and low need for peer approval—and is unwilling to reorient his or her life toward a new goal—low goal flexibility.

An important point about the rating of the dimensions is that the process is judgmental. There are no immediate scores available from any of the exercises, only narrative reports. Even where there are quantitative data, no precise formulas are provided, so that each assessor can weigh the importance of the various pieces of data at hand.

Techniques. The techniques used in an assessment center vary from one application to another. One thing they do have in common, in order to qualify as an assessment center (Task Force on Development of Assessment Center Standards, 1977), is one or more simulations. Here the principle is to use samples, not signs, of behavior (Wernimont and Campbell, 1968) for the manifestation of certain important managerial skills. A favorite example of a management simulation is the in-basket, originally developed for AT&T by Educational Testing Service (ETS) as a training device. This exercise presents the participant with a variety of letters, memos, records of telephone calls, and reports that might be found in the in-basket of a manager whose job the center is designed to fill. Actions taken by the assessee during the in-basket simulation must be justified later in an interview with an assessor.

Business games may also be used as assessment center simulations. In one early Management Progress Study exercise called the manufacturing problem, assessees in groups of six were asked to represent a company involved in the manufacture of toys and jointly decide what to produce as market conditions changed. Group discussions are also common simulations. These are usually leaderless, sometimes with assigned roles to defend and other times completely open in format. An example of an assigned role group discussion, again from the early Bell System research, is the promotion problem. Here each assessee must give an oral presentation in support of an assigned candidate. This is followed by a group discussion in which a joint decision must be made on which candidate to select for an available promotion.

Not all asssessment center exercises are simulations. The Bell System research centers include an in-depth interview; tests of mental ability and knowledge of current affairs; projective exercises such as six cards from the Thematic Apperception Test and two incomplete sentences tests; several personality and motivation questionnaires such as the Edwards Personal Preference Schedule, the Guilford-Martin Inventory of Factors (GAMIN) or Guilford-Zimmerman Temperament Survey, the California Psychological Inventory, the Bass version of the California F-scale measure of authoritarianism, and the Sarnoff measure of upward mobility desires; essay questions to evaluate writing skills and content; a Q-sort measure of self-concept; and some additional questionnaires of expectations and experiences.

Assessors. More than one assessor is required to staff an assessment center to provide greater reliability of judgment. A typical staff might consist of an assessor for every three assessees, or four assessors to observe the usual group of twelve assessees.

The assessors have three major functions. First, they observe the simulations and other exercises that produce no immediately quantifiable scores. Observations of group exercises are usually done by a pair of assessors, while interviews are conducted one-on-one between assessor and assessee. The assessors next write reports of what they have observed; these are composed in a narrative style, describing how each person behaved in the exercise. A final task is to evaluate the information presented from all exercises and test scores at a final integration session. Each exercise report and score is read aloud and the assessors independently rate each dimension. The dimension ratings are then recited aloud by each assessor, and any disagreement of two points or more on a five-point scale is resolved by discussion.

The research assessment centers require three days for assessee observation, another three days for report writing, and two hours per assessee to complete the integration process. Obviously, the assessment center method is neither fast nor inexpensive. Still, the Bell System research represents the Cadillac of assessments; other operational centers take place in as little time as one day.

Before leaving the subject of the assessment center components, it should be pointed out that the method in some ways seems to be counter to scientific psychology (Howard, 1974). The techniques vary widely, including many whose validity is not well established for managerial selection. Much of the evidence is unquantified, there are no fixed rules for how clinical judgment should be applied, and even the dimensions are defined only briefly. Moreover, in operational assessment centers, laypersons are called upon to make difficult judgments that many psychologists would argue about. Still, there is strong evidence that in spite of its vulnerabilities, the assessment center method pulls its disparate parts into a coherent picture, so that predicted managerial success is later borne out in fact. To give an example of some of this evidence, let us turn to the Bell System's Management Progress Study.

The Management Progress Study

Although conceptualized in the 1950s as a short-range study of the development of young managers, the Management Progress Study (MPS) continues today as a comprehensive, longitudinal study of the lives and careers of managers in the Bell System. The study remains a confidential basic research project. No data on individuals has ever been fed back to company officials.

Those involved in the study are white males from six telephone companies who are now middle-aged and in mid or late career stages. The purpose of the study as originally stated were to find out: (1) what significant changes take place in men as their lives develop in a business context; (2) what changes that might be expected or desired do not occur; (3) the causes of observed changes and stabilities, particularly the effects of company climate, policies, and practices; and (4) how accurately and with what indicators progress in management can be predicted.

The design of the study in its completed phases is shown in Table 1. Participants in the MPS sample are of two types. There were 274 new college graduates hired by the Bell System operating companies into the first level of management and 148 persons, not college graduates upon hire, who had begun their careers in the nonmanagement ranks in such positions as telephone installers. All of the noncollege men had been promoted into management by the time they were thirty-two years of age and thus became rivals to the college group for higher level management jobs.

Table 1. Management Progress Study Design and Sample

Year		Sample Size		
		College	Noncollege	Total
0	*Assessment*	274	148	422
1–7	Annual interviews with participants, company			
	Annual Expectations and attitude questionnaires			
8	*Reassessment*	167	142	309
10–19	Triannual interviews with participants, bosses, and terminators			
	Triannual biographical questionnaires			
20	*MPS: 20 assessment* (Midlife and midcareer)	137	129	266

The first year, called Year 0 in Table 1, covered a span of five calendar years from 1956 to 1960. The assessment centers were run only during the summer months since academic psychologists were available during that time as staff assessors. In the seven years that followed, personal interviews of about two hours each were conducted annually with each participant. Independent interviews were conducted with company representatives about the persons involved. Telephone interviews were conducted with those who had left the Bell System. In the eighth year of the study, reassessment was conducted in which the assessees went through another three days of tests and exercises the same as or parallel to the ones they had undertaken in the original assessment phase.

Following the reassessment, the interview schedule was changed to every three years, with independent interviews of participants and their bosses, and telephone interviews with those who had terminated their employment with the company. At Year 20, the men were brought back to another assessment center, although this time the repetition of exercises took only one day. The remaining two days were devoted to new exercises developed to explore middle life and mid-career. This phase of the study occurred in the 1970s. As the drama of the male mid-life crisis crowded the popular literature, AT&T took an in-depth look at such issues with a sample of men on whom there was already a considerable amount of historical information. Data collection continues for the Management Progress Study, with interviews held on five-year basis. A new category of participant is the retiree. It is hoped that this phase of life can be explored more intently at still another assessment center in the thirty-fifth year of the study.

As the study progressed, there have been periodic examinations of how the original assessment center predictions of managerial success compared to the actual progress of the men in Bell System management. At the time of the twentieth year reassessment (dubbed MPS:20), 266 men were still employed in the Bell System and actively involved in the study. Their distribution across the seven levels of operating telephone company management is shown in Table 2. Among the college graduates, the modal or typical management level was the third level, or the entry to middle management. Thirty-one percent had advanced even higher, including three to vice president, or the sixth level. Among the noncollege men, the typical level was the second level, while 32 percent had done better. None of these men had risen above the fourth level by the MPS:20 assessment, reflecting ability differences and some degree of favoritism toward the college men for promotions.

The original predictions of managerial success were made at the assessment centers following achievement of consensus on the ratings of the dimensions. The critical prediction question was "Will this man make the third level of management within ten years?" The selection of ten years was somewhat arbitrary, but was thought to represent a reasonable amount of time for a high potential manager to be moved from the first to the third level. What the staff was really rating was potential for higher management jobs. A vote of "yes" by the majority of the staff meant the person was seen as having high potential, while a vote of "no" meant he did not seem to have high potential. Where the staff was fairly evenly divided in their opinions, a "?" rating was given.

Comparisons of the men's actual progress after eight or ten years showed a considerable degree of accuracy for the original predictions. These results have held up to a great extent even after twenty years of job experience. Table 3 shows the original predictions or indicators of managerial potential and the number who advanced further than the modal persons in the study. Among college men, 43 percent rated favorably at the original assessment center had been advanced to the fourth level or beyond, the modal college level being the third level. This compared favorably to high advancement for

Table 2. Management Levels at MPS: 20

	College		Noncollege	
	N	*%*	*N*	*%*
Level 6	3	2%	0	0%
5	12	9%	0	0%
4	27	20%	4	3%
3	64	40%	37	29%
2	4	3%	61	47%
1	4	3%	27	21%
Total	137	100%	129	100%

Table 3. Assessment Predictions and Attainment
of More than Modal Level

Prediction of Third Level in 10 Years	N	College Attained Fourth Level or Higher in 20 Years		N	Noncollege Attained Third Level or Higher in 20 Years	
		N	%		N	%
Yes	63	27	43%	36	21	58%
No and ?	74	15	20%	93	20	22%
Total	137	42	31%	129	41	32%

only 20 percent of those who had not been seen as having high potential at the center. Among the noncollege men, whose modal level was the second, the third level or higher was attained by 58 percent of those rated favorably at assessment and by only 22 percent of those who were not. Thus the research data demonstrate that the assessment center was able to identify those destined for managerial success. This occurred in conditions of confidentiality; the information was not used to bias the outcomes of the men's careers.

Factors and Exercises Predicting Managerial Success

If the assessment center method is a good predictor of managerial success, it is important to know exactly what makes it work. What managerial characteristics are important and how are those characteristics best measured?

To answer the first part of the question, we can examine some empirical data on the characteristics that best predict managerial success after a twenty-year period. The relative weight of different dimensions or clusters of dimensions depends somewhat on the time period of measurement and the relative management levels and ages of the participants. Prediction was most accurate in the early years of the study, before experience, personal development, and other circumstances began to alter the equations. Nevertheless, evidence is offered here for the long-range prediction over twenty years.

Table 4 shows the correlation of each of the assessment dimension factors or clusters of dimensions with the level attained at MPS:20. Some of the factors originally found important to success began to lose their import over a twenty-year period of time. For example, being independent of others signalled early career success, but as the years passed and most of the men became more independent-minded (Bray and Howard, 1983), that factor no longer showed a relationship with achieved management level. Stability of performance, as measured at the original assessment, also declined in predictive power over time. Work involvement was significantly related to success to only a small degree.

Table 4. Assessment Factors Predicting MPS: 20 Level

	r With Level
Administrative Skills	.19**
Interpersonal Skills	.22**
Intellectual Ability	.25**
Stability of Performance	.12
Work Involvement	.15*
Advancement Motivation	.28**
Independence of Others	.00

$*p < .05$, $**p < .005$

The remaining four factors in Table 4 did show fairly strong relationships to success, especially considering the length of time over which the prediction was made. In order of size of correlation, although the size differences are not necessarily statistically significant, the most potent predictor was advancement motivation. The degree to which a man wanted to succeed early in his career played a strong role in determining whether or not he would succeed. Intellectual ability was also an important factor, followed by interpersonal skills and administrative skills.

The exercises that contributed to the dimension ratings for each of the most important factors are shown in Tables 5 through 8. Only data considered by the assessment staff in making the respective dimension ratings are included, even though other exercise scores may also be correlated with the factor. Many of the exercises did not produce immediately quantifiable results, but later coding of many of them attached numerical values to the qualitative data the assessors were responding to in the integration sessions. The interview, business game, leaderless group discussion, and the in-basket simulation were rated on fifteen to eighteen dimensions each, paralleling the definitions of the assessment dimensions. In addition, the interviews were coded for nine life themes (Rychlak, 1982), and the projective tests on nine special scales (Grant, Katkovsky, and Bray, 1967).

The administrative skills factor was rated in the most straightforward way. As shown in Table 5, the in-basket simulation was the primary exercise used to rate the dimensions of organizing and planning, and decision making. As shown by the multiple correlation, in-basket decision making, organizing and planning, and the overall rating contributed some independent variance in the prediction of the factor.

Table 6 shows that two simulations, the promotion problem and the manufacturing problem, were primarily used by the assessors in their ratings of the dimensions in the interpersonal skills factor. Leadership skills, as observed in the promotion problem, was the most potent predictor of this factor, but the observation of leadership skills in the manufacturing problem accounted for additional variance. Thus, the exact same behavior was not pro-

Table 5. Administrative Skills Factor Correlations
with Exercises Considered by Assessors

Source	Exercise Score	r	Mult R*
In-Basket	Decision-Making	.74	.74
In-Basket	Organizing and Planning	.68	.78
In-Basket	Overall Rating	.74	.79

*Multiple R shown only where variable makes significant contribution at $p < .05$. MPS assessment data, $N = 336$.

duced by each exercise. Also augmenting the prediction were the overall ratings on both the oral presentation and group discussion parts of the promotion problem discussion and observations of behavior flexibility in the manufacturing problem.

In contrast to the heavy use of simulations for the preceding two factors, paper-and-pencil tests were the primary tools used to evaluate the intellectual ability factor, shown in Table 7. The verbal section of the SCAT test carried the most weight, although the quantitative portion also added to the prediction. Both the contemporary affairs test and the critical thinking tests, though highly intercorrelated with the SCAT, added some independent variance, as did a rating of range of interests from the interview.

The most complex of the four major factors in terms of evidence used to rate it was the advancement motivation factor, shown in Table 8. A combination of interview, projectives, and personality test data were used to make judgments about this factor. The rating of need for advancement from the interview was the strongest predictor. Predictive power was significantly increased by adding low need for security and the financial acquisitive life theme coded from the interview; preference for a leadership role and achievement/advancement motivation coded from the projective reports; general activity from the GAMIN personality inventory; and the total score from the Sarnoff questionnaire of upward mobility drive.

Table 6. Interpersonal Skills Factor Correlations
with Exercises Considered by Assessors

Source	Exercise Score	r	Mult R*
Promotion Problem	Leadership Skills	.64	.64
Manufacturing Problem	Leadership Skills	.40	.72
Promotion Problem	Overall Rating	.56	.74
Manufacturing Problem	Behavior Flexibility	.37	.76
Promotion Problem	Oral Presentation	.46	.78

*Multiple R shown only where variable makes significant contribution at $p < .05$. MPS assessment data, $N = 114$.

Table 7. Intellectual Ability Factor Correlations
with Exercises Considered by Assessors

Source	Exercise Score	r	Mult R^*
SCAT	Verbal	.77	.77
Test	Contemporary Affairs	.66	.83
SCAT	Quantitative	.48	.84
Interview	Range of Interests	.30	.85
Test	Critical Thinking	.67	.85

*Multiple R shown only where variable makes significant contribution at $p < .05$. MPS assessment data, $N = 336$.

In summary, the four major factors found to contribute to managerial success within the Management Progress Study were each primarily measured by different techniques in the assessment center. Although cognitive tests were invaluable in evaluating intellectual ability, administrative skills were best measured in the in-basket; interpersonal skills in the two group exercises; and advancement motivation from the interview, projective tests, and personality questionnaires. It appears that a variety of such exercises is needed to tap the major components of a complex job like that of the manager.

The Case of Roland

To drive home the point about the need for multiple measures of managerial ability and motivation, let us consider a case study. The participant is from the Management Continuity Study, the second Bell System longitudianal study begun in 1977 to parallel the Management Progress Study with a new generation of Bell System managers (Howard and Bray, 1981). Roland (not his real name) made a very forceful impression in the assessment center interview. His father was successful business executive in the Midwest and his

Table 8. Advancement Motivation Factor Correlations
with Exercises Considered by Assessors

Source	Exercise Score	r	Mult R^*
Interview	Need for Advancement	.65	.65
Projectives	Leadership Role	.44	.70
GAMIN	General Activity	.43	.73
Interview	Need for Security	− .47	.74
Interview	Financial-Acquisitive Life Theme	.36	.75
Projectives	Achievement/Advancement Motivation	.44	.76
Sarnoff	Total-Upward Mobility Drive	.28	.77

*Multiple R shown only where variable makes significant contribution at $p < .05$. MPS assessment data, $N = 274$.

mother was a schoolteacher. Both were intelligent and very demanding of Roland, so that he incorporated the value of working hard and dissatisfaction with being anything but the best. He pushed himself in high school to high academic performance and active participation in extracurricular activities in order to get accepted to a good college. He achieved this goal and was a serious student as well as a campus leader in a small, well-regarded private college, where he graduated with a 3.4 average.

Roland was recruited to a Bell System operating company in his senior year of college and joined shortly after graduation. He had been on his job of business office supervisor for three months when he attended the AT&T research assessment center. He told the interviewer quite flatly that he intended to become the president of the operating company. He knew it would require a lot of hard work and claimed he was already putting in a ten- to twelve-hour day. He hoped to be in middle management within five years and at the assistant vice-president–level within ten years. This was extremely ambitious by Bell System standards, but he seemed determined to do it.

Roland's personality questionnaires and projectives verified his strong motivation to succeed. His Sarnoff score showed him to be at the ninety-first percentile of Bell Systems norms on need for upward mobility. The Edwards Personal Preference Schedule found him very high on dominance, achievement, endurance, and aggression. According to the Guilford-Zimmerman Temperament Survey, he was high on general activity, ascendance, sociability, and emotional stability, all characteristics that would serve him well on a rise to the top. His SCAT verbal score was somewhat disappointing, at the thirty-fourth percentile of Bell System college norms, but he had an average knowledge of current affairs and had indicated by his college grades that he would probably work long and hard to master those things that did not come to him quickly.

The typical selection procedure for a manager would probably have stopped at this point and put Roland on a fast-track program to managerial success. His advancement motivation was exceptionally high, his cognitive test scores were acceptable, and he had demonstrated leadership in several college activities. But the assessment center criterion is not satisfied by these few techniques, and Roland was put through several simulations.

Roland's professed competitive drive was only sporadically shown in the competitive group discussion and his performance was lackluster. Given ten minutes to present his case for funds to a mock city council, he took only two minutes. He said nothing particularly interesting, but merely repeated vaguely some of the material on his fact sheet, mixing in a series of mangled cliches. His speech was innocuous, easy to ignore, and seemed to have little impact on the group. His participation in the group discussion that followed was minimal, ineffective, and immature. He displayed some competitive style when he attacked two other group members on their facts, but he did not pursue his points and did little to counter their arguments for funds for their own causes. He had little effect on the resolution of the problem; the department he was representing received nothing. He did little better in the noncompetitive group discussion, which simulated a community counseling center. He was superficial in his understanding of the cases and tried to seek attention with poorly developed jokes and boisterous behavior.

In the in-basket exercise, his organization and planning was significantly hindered by carelessness and inattention. He was vague and forgetful about his decision to attend an out-of-town business conference on his first official day on the job and kept confusing the name of the subordinate he planned to take with him. He was not simply inattentive to detail but also careless in thinking through the organizational issues and relationships with which he was involved. For example, he left instructions to a replacement secretary to tell not only his equals and subordinates but also his superiors to "jump when he snapped" with respect to a questionable meeting he had set up.

His uncertainty extended to many of his decisions. During the in-basket interview, he could not remember to whom he had delegated several memos; his reasons for delegating were often unclear even when he could remember. His attitude toward others in the exercise was often high-handed. He indicated a willingness to fire more than one individual on the basis of very little information. The overall impression created by his in-basket was that he would be not only ineffective in the job but also unlikely to endear himself to most in his organization. After hearing all the evidence on Roland, the staff rated him a poor candidate for higher management in the Bell System.

This case is not a typical one in an assessment center, for we are usually comforted by the consistencies we find with deliberate redundancies in information obtained. It clearly illustrates that paper-and-pencil tests and an interview are frequently not enough information on which to base a sound judgment about managerial abilities and motivation. The precaution is sounded to believe what candidates do and not just what they say. The opportunity to do this is one reason the Bell System and thousands of other organizations shore up promotion recommendations with management assessment centers.

References

Bray, D. W., and Grant, D. L. "The Assessment Center in the Measurement of Potential for Business Management." *Psychological Monographs,* 1966, *80* (17), entire issue.

Bray, D. W., and Howard, A. "The AT&T Longitudinal Studies of Managers." In K. W. Schaie (Ed.), *Longitudinal Studies of Adult Psychological Development.* New York: Guilford Press, 1983.

Grant, D. L., Katkovsky, W., and Bray, D. W. "Contributions of Projective Techniques to Assessment of Management Potential." *Journal of Applied Psychology,* 1967, *51,* 226–232.

Howard, A. "An Assessment of Assessment Centers." *Academy of Management Journal,* 1974, *17* (1), 115–134.

Howard, A., and Bray, D. W. "Today's Young Managers: They Can Do It But Will They?" *Wharton Magazine,* 1981, *5* (4), 23–28.

Murray, H. A. *Explorations in Personality.* New York: Oxford University Press, 1938.

Office of Strategic Services. Assessment Staff. *Assessment of Men.* New York: Rinehart, 1948.

Rychlak, J. S. *Personality and Life Style of Young Male Managers: A Logical Learning Theory Analysis.* New York: Academic Press, 1982.

Task Force on Development of Assessment Center Standards. In J. L. Moses and W. C. Byham (Eds.), *Applying the Assessment Center Method.* New York: Pergamon Press, 1977.

Wernimont, P. F., and Campbell, J. P. "Signs, Samples, and Criteria." *Journal of Applied Psychology,* 1968, *52,* 372–376.

Ann Howard is division manager of basic human resources research for the American Telephone and Telegraph Company. Her major responsibility is directing the research for the two ongoing comprehensive longitudinal studies of managers referred to in this chapter.

*Attempts to measure personal qualities in admissions are often
inadequate because of poor understanding of the admissions process.
Results of a major study illustrate the different objectives in
admissions and how use of personal qualities might be improved.*

Measuring Personal Qualities in Admissions: The Context and the Purpose

Warren W. Willingham

In admitting their students, colleges and universities ordinarily give primary attention to academic qualifications; they also consider a variety of such personal qualities as leadership, special talents, background characteristics, or career interests. What role such qualities play and should play in admissions has always been unclear and is frequently debated.

In a traditional research approach to this problem, one might develop a measure of motivation, character, extracurricular achievement, or whatever; plug it into a regression equation with high school rank and test score; and determine to what extent the new measure improves prediction of grade point average or some other measure of success. Many such efforts have foundered over the past thirty years because of disappointing validity, ethical problems in using the measure, impracticality, and so on.

This is perhaps an overdrawn scenario, but it is certainly true that we have been far more successful with aptitude and achievement tests than with the so-called soft measures that may be pertinent to college admissions. An important reason, I believe, is that we have a poor understanding of the admissions process and how it works. On this issue, there is quite a gulf be-

R. B. Ekstrom (Ed.). *Measurement, Technology, and Individuality in Education.* New Directions for Testing
and Measurement, no. 17. San Francisco: Jossey-Bass, March 1983.

tween measurement specialists and the people who actually are engaged in admissions work.

My thesis is that conventional approaches to measuring and evaluating personal qualities in admissions are often inadequate or inappropriate because we do not pay sufficient attention to the purpose of the measures and the context in which they are used. We need a broader view of the admissions process. I would like to suggest some different perspectives and examine the measurement implications, but first it will be useful to provide some background. I and a number of colleagues are currently involved in a cooperative study of personal qualities in admissions sponsored by the College Board and Educational Testing Service (ETS). A·brief summary of a few initial findings will be useful in illustrating later points.

The Personal Qualities Project

The Personal Qualities Project is an extended effort to determine how a variety of student characteristics are related to actual decisions in the admissions process and to students' later success and experience. A group of nine selective private colleges were asked to join in the study because their exclusive use of the Common Application Form provided a common data base. They were Bucknell University, Colgate University, Hartwick College, Kalamazoo College, Kenyon College, Occidental College, Ohio Wesleyan University, University of Richmond, and Williams College. The specific findings cannot be generalized beyond the types of institutions represented, although many of the issues we are studying apply to most colleges and universities.

The study focuses on three types of personal qualities. First, there are background characteristics such as age, sex, ethnicity, socioeconomic factors, place of residence, and affiliation with the institution. Background factors are especially important for their social and economic implications.

Second, there are personal achievements in such areas as leadership, athletics, community service, or in creative endeavors like art, music, writing, science, drama, and so on. Indicators include public recognition, awards, offices, and recommendations. A significant personal achievement can be manifested as an unusual accomplishment or a highly developed skill. It is personal because it represents an optional commitment of effort outside the normal demands of the formal course of study and routine assignments of grades. It can be cognitive, affective, or physical. Significant achievements have special social value in fostering individual development and the ability to perform competently in real-life situations.

Third, a student's goals and interests represent a type of personal quality that often plays a critical role in admissions. We have focused upon practical issues such as what course of study is followed, what are the intended career plans, and what particular educational goals in college are most important to the student. One can think of these three types of personal qualities as where I came from, what I have accomplished, and what I want to do.

Starting in December of 1978, admissions data were collected on some 25,000 applicants to the nine colleges. The 5,000 who enrolled in the fall of 1979 are being followed for four years. Breland and I described project results obtained through the freshman year in a book published this past spring by the College Board (Willingham and Breland, 1982), but it will be another two years before the final results of the study are reported. These are selected reflections from midstream, so to speak.

The proportion of applicants accepted varied widely at these nine institutions, but each college placed primary emphasis on academic factors, as was its stated policy intention. Overall, the colleges' academic ratings of the applicant folders received about three times as much weight as the personal ratings in predicting admissions decisions. The two main academic factors—high school rank and test scores—were weighted about equally. These two measures predicted admissions decisions fairly well, but there was no indication that any of these colleges was using a cutoff score on academic measures.

In order to examine the effect of personal qualities on selection decisions, residual selection rates were computed for a number of different characteristics, that is, the actual selection rate for a particular type of student minus the selection rate that would be expected on the basis of the high school rank and test scores alone. A number of interesting facts emerged from this analysis.

1. Personal qualities played a greater role in decisions at the most selective colleges and a lesser role at colleges that rejected fewer applicants.

2. Minority status had the largest residual selection rate, indicating strong affirmative action in admissions decisions, although minority representation was not large in these institutions.

3. Other background characteristics with positive rates included alumni ties and residence—local commuters as well as those from a distant state. The data indicate that, overall, socially privileged groups did not receive preference in selection decisions. Moreover, a student's application for financial aid did not influence the admissions decision.

4. Contrary to what is generally thought, outstanding curricular accomplishments in leadership, athletics, community service, and creative activities had little effect on selection.

5. Coming to the campus for an interview did not, in itself, enhance the likelihood of acceptance, but in some colleges those applicants with high interview ratings were more likely to be accepted than their academic achievement or other qualities would indicate.

6. Several important outcomes of selection, the last two results in particular, were notably inconsistent with the institutions' publicly stated admissions policy and came as a surprise to the colleges.

We got especially interesting results when residual analyses were carried out separately for those applicants who had high, uncertain, or low likelihoods of acceptance on the basis of high school rank and test scores. As we suspected, personal qualities did not often come into play when acceptance was likely. On the other hand, significant personal achievement and outstanding references did seem to be used as tie breakers among students with similar academic credentials in the "uncertain" category. Some background characteristics, such as alumni ties and minority status, had a strong positive effect in both the "unlikely" and "uncertain" categories.

While there were variations among the colleges, overall the validity of high school rank and test scores as grade predictors was equal and corresponded to their relative weight in selection; personal measures were not a useful supplement or substitute for the academic measures in predicting grades. Personal achievement measures were usually better predictors of which freshmen would be nominated by their peers as having had a successful first year. College ratings of applicants were usually not helpful in predicting freshman grades, but these ratings were useful in predicting the peer nomination criterion. Persistence to the sophomore year was unpredictable on the basis of any preadmission measures. For the great bulk of the students, retention seemed more related to the student's sense of progress toward personal goals than to academic performance in colleges.

In gathering data from seniors, we are taking pains to construct criteria that represent different types of success that are valued by the college. Meanwhile, what measurement implications can be drawn from this work to date? I return now to my thesis concerning the importance of context and of purpose.

The Context — Diverse Admissions Procedures

When personal qualities are used in admissions, clearly the assumption is that the college is thereby accomplishing certain desirable ends. If, following Messick (1980), we are to examine the evidential and consequential basis for their validity — that is, find out how the measures are working — we must have an adequate understanding of the admissions process. Our present understanding of that process is not adequate in two respects.

First, we often assume that admissions means only selection, forgetting that students make decisions to apply and matriculate. This results in a narrow view of which student characteristics are relevant and deserve study. Furthermore, it can be argued that the essential function of admissions is to maintain enrollment of an appropriate student body. Enrollment maintenance must also include retention and is therefore the net effect of four processes.

1. *Application*—based on student self-selection, as influenced by the college image and its recruitment efforts.
2. *Selection*—based on institutional decisions, but likely to offer limited options to most colleges over the next decade.
3. *Matriculation*—based on the student's decision to enroll, which is difficult for the college to predict or influence in individual cases.
4. *Retention*—mostly student decisions and probably based more on personal than academic considerations.

The administrative objective of this process is to maintain appropriate enrollment; the educational objective should be to improve students' educational choices and enhance their individual development. Both objectives bear upon educational effectiveness and are important to all institutions, not just the selective ones.

A second problem in understanding the context is knowing how selection actually works. Several selection models can be distinguished.

Academic Prediction. This is the conventional strategy of selecting the students most likely to make good grades, on the basis of previous academic record and test scores. The predictive model can be based, of course, on a variety of success criteria. It can be applied generally across an institution or selectively within, and tailored to individual programs.

Mosaic. This model is a multiple quota strategy for filling a number of important cells in the freshman class that might not be adequately represented if students are selected on academic credentials alone. That is, the college wants to be be sure to admit an adequate number of women, minority students, alumni legacies, hockey players, chemistry majors, applicants from key feeder schools, and so on. This model evidently influences selection in many colleges, particularly in the private sector (see Moll, 1979). In pure form, it might be described as a series of separate races where the most able students are selected within each category until each quota is filled—in which case the model is probably unconstitutional, in light of the Bakke decision.

Group Equity. This consists of a family of models that are mainly intended to provide value bases for defining what proportion of various groups, especially minority and majority, should be admitted (Thorndike, 1971; Cole, 1973). The group equity model can be viewed as a special case of the mosaic, although probably no such model exists in practice. Equity models have been questioned on several grounds (Petersen and Novick, 1976); their constitutionality is also suspect.

Poker Chip. In this system, all applicants run one race, but get a specified number of chips for demonstrated levels of competence, certain background characteristics, or any other personal quality important to the college. Students are admitted if their stacks of chips reach a designated level. This model can be expressed, of course, as an admissions equation with weights for the various factors resulting in a composite admissions index. It differs from the academic prediction model not only in incorporating different types of measures, but also in the fact that some of the weights are set a priori, and there is not necessarily any single criterion against which the composite can be statistically validated in any conventional sense.

Two-Stage. The two-stage model was recommended by the Carnegie Council on Policy Studies (Manning, 1977). The institution first sets a standard for admissibility at the minimum level at which evidence indicates that a student is likely to succeed. Second, the institution selects from among those judged admissible, using a variety of personal characteristics that serve to advance the institution's educational objectives.

Special Admissions. This system has been used by some public institutions (for example, the University of California) to admit most of their students according to a mandated formula based on grade record and test scores, but allowing a small percentage to be admitted on administrative "chits," which may be earmarked to serve particular purposes as well as provide some administrative flexibility for handling unusual individual cases.

Contingency. The contingency model is based on multiple considerations, which vary depending on the particular characteristics of the applicant. For example, applicants with high test scores and grade records are selected unless their patterns of coursework are notably poor and the weaknesses are not compensated by minority or alumni ties. An applicant with middling grades would be accepted only if there is an unusual accomplishment on his or her record and if the student also helps to fill some other admissions target associated with a particular feeder school or college major. An applicant with low grades would be unlikely to be accepted, despite an unusual accomplishment or strong school reference, unless he has some particular quality—for example, special athletic proficiency, or minority or alumni ties—that the college wants but has been unable to select from among better-qualified applicants.

Observe that each of the subsequent models builds on the academic prediction model by incorporating procedural variations in order to take into account personal qualities of students. In each case, the apparent intention is to get around the fact that the conventional academic prediction model does not fit the selection strategies of the institution very well. Nowhere is this more obvious than in the last model, which best describes selection practices of the more selective colleges in the Personal Qualities Project. This contingency model reflects an effort to achieve a number of objectives, often competing or unrelated, some of which may become apparent only in the course of the selection process. Needless to say, it would be useful to learn more about such models and how they work.

The Purpose—Serving Diverse Institutional Objectives

In evaluating the appropriateness and usefulness of personal qualities in admissions, the central issue is the intrinsic validity of the process: Does the process serve the purposes intended, and are the purposes defensible? The admissions policy and practices of a particular college are justified because its constituents—faculty, trustees, alumni, and legislature—consider the overall process to be reasonably fair and effective from both an educational and a social point of view. As we know, admissions policy is a frequent battleground where practices are often the result of poltical compromise. The reason is that there are multiple purposes and values in admissions; that is, there are varieties of effectiveness and fairness. For example, when an institution selects those students whom it considers likely to succeed academically, it might also give preference to students:

- Who have special talents or career-related skills that may be needed either in college or later in order to succeed in a particular field
- Who can make a unique contribution to a pluralistic learning environment because of their cultural backgrounds, interests, or experiences
- Who can serve special needs of the institution because of their special competence—as a first violinist or a quarterback—or because their educational plans fit institutional priorities
- Who have demonstrated unusual initiative or some concrete accomplishment that deserves recognition and reward
- Whose backgrounds serve to strengthen important ties with constituents such as alumni, the local community, professional associations, or feeder schools
- Who show special potential for nonacademic development valued by the institution in areas such as leadership, social service, or entrepreneurship.

Several aspects of this list are worth noting. A wide variety of personal qualities are used to serve quite diverse purposes in selection. More important, in each of these examples, it does not necessarily follow that the purpose is to select students who are expected to excel academically. That is usually not the objective. These uses of personal qualities are sanctioned not because they improve prediction of grades but because they foster individual development, help the institution, or have some other beneficial effect. Note also that these various characteristics do not apply to all students; they are not normally justified on their own as bases for selection but, rather, as one set of a number of qualities considered along with evidence of academic competence (Bowen, 1977; Manning, 1977; Powell, 1978).

In justifying the use of personal qualities, it is certainly correct to ask whether an empirical study would be useful, and if so, what criteria are appropriate. It is also correct to ask what other considerations justify using the measure, with how much weight, and in what circumstances. Finally, it is critical to ask whether selection practice conforms with intended policy. In the Personal Qualities Project, this was often not the case.

Looking critically at how colleges use personal qualities demonstrates particularly well that validation in selective admissions is primarily a rational procedure that takes account of the purpose of the process and the likely effects of carrying it out in a particular way with a particular combination of measures (Willingham, 1976). Empirical facts are necessary in order to evaluate technical assumptions and understand the actual outcome of the process, but if we measurement specialists occupy ourselves singlemindedly with predictive validity, we are likely to miss the point of much of what goes on in the admissions process.

Another way to get a useful perspective on the purposes personal qualities can serve in admissions is to examine their strengths and weaknesses. The strengths tend to broaden one's view of useful purposes; the weaknesses impose limitations.

The compelling advantage in assessing personal qualities in admissions is obvious. This broadened view of applicants helps to serve better the individuality of students, the multiple purposes of education, and the diverse needs of society. In a now classic essay, Gardner (1961) argued the social value of different forms of excellence. He used this homily: If we blindly honor mediocre philosophy at the expense of good plumbing, neither our pipes nor our philosophies will hold water.

Another strength in assessing personal qualities is the inherent value in recognizing productive accomplishment and subsequent individual development. When colleges act on evidence that students have done something outstanding, a helpful message is sent back to students and schools.

Finally, admissions is a point of transition when we should be doing what we can to help students direct themselves, connect with educational programs and career possibilities, and otherwise get themselves organized. In dealing with these matters, it is hardly adequate to rely only on such cognitive measures as grades and admissions tests, useful though these may be.

We are well aware that there are serious weaknesses in many measures of personal qualities. Subjective judgments can be quite unreliable, subject to bias and distortion, and inaccurate for various reasons. Students' backgrounds are not always comparable, nor do different students provide information with the same degree of objectivity and candor.

And there are ethical hazards. Invasion of privacy is one. Another is the possibility of introducing systematic biases or prejudices of exactly the sort tests were designed to avoid. There are subtle dangers of personalism that can infringe on the rights of individuals, or cause them to be judged harshly for spurious reasons. These are not trivial technical problems or exaggerated worries. They are fundamental issues concerned with fairness and validity.

The question is how to build on the strengths and reduce the hazards. Let me close by suggesting several areas of research and development that I believe need more attention. One I have already emphasized—the need to develop a better understanding of the admissions process and how measures are actually used in reaching decisions that accomplish multiple objectives. Practitioners need better devices to monitor the process and determine whether practices are yielding the outcomes desired. I believe that could be done without great difficulty by using an adaptation of the residual model described here.

A second, related, need is to work toward a better understanding of professional — or, as we might say, subjective — judgment. There have been useful lines of research on such topics as paramorphic representation and statistical versus clinical prediction, but, at present, subjective judgment seems to involve complex and important decisions that we do not comprehend very well. What do we know of the broader role of professional judgment in incorporating values, in protecting against those few decisions that may be statistically correct but ethically wrong, in avoiding subtle correlated errors in routine statistical decisions, or in balancing a number of contingencies, some of which may be difficult to anticipate?

It should be possible to identify the most common errors and biases that may distort judgment in the selection process. To some extent, these errors could be avoided by better structuring the judgment. In other words, I think we can and should do a better job of balancing the strengths and shortcomings of professional and statistical decision making.

Self-assessment is a third ambiguous area much in need of conceptual and practical development. Student choices play an important role in admissions, broadly conceived. We like to say that individuals must make informed decisions and assume responsibility for their educational and career planning. But the typical student has a very limited basis for assessing the significance of his or her experience and accomplishments, has limited access to good advice, and usually has a difficult time identifying alternatives and developing plans. I believe that improved measurement of personal qualities for this aspect of the admissions process depends to a considerable extent on advancement in our expertise and instrumentation in self-assessment.

All of these suggestions involve, in one way or another, the problem of improving the interpretation and use of information — test scores as well as other measures that affect people's lives. Given the social concerns about testing in recent years and our continuing effort to improve measurement practice, it is a fitting emphasis.

References

Bowen, W. G. *Princeton Alumni Weekly,* September 26, 1977.

Cole, N. S. "Bias in Selection." *Journal of Educational Measurement,* 1973, *10,* 237–255.

Gardner, J. W. *Excellence — Can We Be Equal and Excellent, Too?* New York: Harper & Row, 1961.

Manning, W. H. "The Pursuit of Fairness in Admissions." In *Selective Admissions in Higher Education,* a report of the Carnegie Council on Policy Studies in Higher Education. San Francisco: Jossey-Bass, 1977.

Messick, S. "Test Validity and the Ethics of Assessment." *American Psychologist,* 1980, *35* (11), 1012–1027.

Moll, R. W. *Playing the Private College Admissions Game.* New York: Times Books, 1979.

Petersen, N. S., and Novick, M. R. "An Evaluation of Some Models for Culture-Fair Selection." *Journal of Educational Measurement,* 1976, *13* (1), 3–29.

Powell, L. F., Jr. Opinion in Regents of the University of California *v.* Bakke, 438 U.S. 265, 98 Ct., 2377, 57 L. Ed. 2d 750 (1978).

Thorndike, R. L. "Concepts of Culture-Fairness." *Journal of Educational Measurement,* 1971, *8,* 63–70.

Willingham, W. W. *Validity and the Graduate Record Examinations Program.* Princeton, N.J.: Educational Testing Service, 1976.

Willingham, W. W., and Breland, H. M. *Personal Qualities and College Admissions.* New York: College Entrance Examination Board, 1982.

Warren W. Willingham is assistant vice-president for program research and a distinguished research scientist at Educational Testing Service. He is director of the personal-qualities-in-admissions project and coauthor of Personal Qualities and College Admissions.

Assessment of experiential learning must be approached in a different way from assessment of learning acquired through the traditional information assimilation mode. New measurement techniques and program models need to be devised to save money and faculty time, while preserving individualization.

Measuring Learning from Life and Work Experience

Pamela J. Tate

In the first sourcebook published in the *New Directions for Experiential Learning* series, Morris Keeton and I defined experiential learning as "learning in which the learner is directly in touch with the realities being studied. It is contrasted with learning in which the learner only reads about, hears about, talks about, or writes about these realities but never comes in contact with them as part of the learning process" (Keeton and Tate, 1978, p. 2). This definition implies that such learning may occur during a learner's enrollment in a college or university — through an internship, a cooperative education placement, or field study — or before the time of enrollment. When the learning occurs off campus in a work setting and is a regular part of the learner's program of study, it is often referred to as college-sponsored experiential learning. When it occurs prior to a learner's enrollment or outside an institution of higher education and is then presented for assessment by college faculty, it is usually called prior experiential learning. Regardless of where or when the learning occurred, it is truly experiential if, as Coleman (1976) suggests, the person has learned not by receiving and processing symbolic information, but by carrying out an action in a work, leisure, or family setting; seeing the effects of that action; arriving at an understanding of a general principle from that particular instance; and applying the learning in a new circumstance.

R. B. Ekstrom (Ed.). *Measurement, Technology, and Individuality in Education.* New Directions for Testing and Measurement, no. 17. San Francisco: Jossey-Bass, March 1983.

Although educators often discuss college-sponsored and prior experiential learning as if they had little in common, I would like to suggest that many of the assessment issues with regard to experiential learning pertain to both the sponsored and prior varieties. In my view, the reasons these two species of experiential learning have been treated as if they were so different have little to do with measurement questions, but much to do with politics, history, financing, faculty perceptions, rationales for program implementation, and the characteristics of the learners who are usually involved in each kind of experiential learning program. This chapter will discuss the common theoretical ground between sponsored and prior learning; the special assessment issues each poses for faculty; and the real-world, practical reasons that prior learning has not yet achieved the same degree of acceptance in the academy as sponsored learning. This chapter will then offer some recommendations for those interested in fostering wider use of both varieties of experiential learning.

To clarify some of the central issues in assessing learning from life and work experience, it is first useful to review Coleman's description of the differences between the information assimilation mode of learning and the experiential. In the information assimilation mode, he tells us, information about a general principle, or examples that serve to illustrate the principle, are transmitted through a symbolic medium such as a lecture or a book. The learner assimilates and organizes the information so that the general principle is understood, infers an application from this general principle, and then applies the knowledge. With regard to the last step, the application stage, Coleman (1976, p. 51) emphasizes that "only when this step has been completed can the person be said to have completed the learning so that the information initially received is useful to him in his everyday action."

The experiential learning process occurs in a very different sequence. It begins with action, with experience. Knowledge of general principles is attained through an inductive process in which the learner understands the consequences of the action in the immediate situation and then is able to discern themes and connections between many similar actions and similar effects. Coleman (1976, p. 52) is careful to point out that, in experiential learning, understanding the general principle does not imply an ability to express the principle in a symbolic medium such as language. "It implies," he says, "only the ability to see a connection between the actions and effects over a range of circumstances."

Adapted from the Council for the Advancement of Experiential Learning (CAEL) Faculty Development Program resource book (1976, p.13-9), Table 1 summarizes the main differences between the two modes.

These characteristics indicate that assessment of experiential learning, whether that learning occurs during a college-sponsored internship for a nineteen-year-old biology major, or as a result of a woman's twenty-year career as

Table 1. Characteristics of Coleman's Two Learning Modes

Information Assimilation Mode	*Experiential Mode*
Process	Process
Information through symbolic communication (lectures, reading)	Information through experience and observation
Understanding through deduction (generalizing first, and then particularizing)	Understanding through induction (particularizing first, and then generalizing)
Application	Reapplication in new situation
Depends heavily on symbolic medium, usually language	Depends on action and observation of concrete events
Depends on artificial or extrinsic motivation, such as grades, because action occurs at end of learning sequence	Motivation is intrinsic because action occurs at beginning of learning sequence
Time-efficient — new principles are presented in crystallized, abstract form	Time-consuming — actions must be repeated enough to generalize from them
Weakness: Learner often has difficulty particularizing and applying	Weakness: Learner often has difficulty generalizing from particular instance

a social service administrator, must be approached in a different way than assessment of learning acquired through the traditional mode. Clearly, experiential learning does not lend itself to assessment procedures such as standardized tests. Since the learning starts with concrete experience and is usually, to use Willingham's (1977, p. 2) phrase, "highly individualized" and quite diverse from student to student, assessment techniques such as performance tests, product assessment, simulation, games, and interviews are likely to be more appropriate than paper-and-pencil examinations.

It is often necessary to use more than one technique and more than one assessor to measure a single learning outcome, particularly when, as Forrest, Knapp, and Pendergrass (1976, p. 169) point out, "a great deal of error is associated with each technique or when the measurement procedures are far removed from direct observation of student performance." For example, if one wished to measure a woman's competence in educational administration, it would not be sufficient to observe her performing on the job. It would be useful to assess written materials she had developed that documented a completed project or plan and to interview her to determine her understanding of organizational theory and higher education policy.

Assessors must also be cautious after inferring that college-level learning has taken place. The assessment must be conducted in such a way that the learner has an opportunity to demonstrate conceptual grasp of the subject matter as well as the ability to apply the knowledge in a new setting. I am familiar with one sociology internship program that places students in juvenile correctional facilities under the supervision of the prison volunteer coordinator and that assesses the students' learning by asking the supervisor to rate the students' job performance. Although the faculty member briefly interviews the students near the end of the experience, there is no systematic questioning of students about their understanding of the criminal justice system. There seems to be an unstated assumption that if the students have been successful in the prison, they must have mastered certain concepts in criminal justice. Yet the learning outcomes have not been assessed. The same assumption is often made in the case of adults requesting credit for prior learning. In one example, a young economics professor at a liberal arts college was confronted with a man who had been vice-president of a major New York bank for twenty-five years and who was claiming knowledge of business administration, finance, banking, and economics. While the bank executive may indeed have mastered those subject areas through his work experience, it was difficult for the faculty member to determine the nature and extent of the learning — a variety of assessment techniques had to be used. I have found that experiential learners are more often adept at doing than at verbally expressing the abstract concepts on which their actions are based. Faculty must keep in mind that, just as learning in the traditional mode is incomplete without the learner reaching the final stage of applying the learning, experiential learning is incomplete without learners attaining a conceptual understanding of the principles underlying their behavior or performance.

Another problem in assessing experiential learning is that since the learning process cannot be monitored or supervised as closely as classroom-based learning — especially in the case of an adult's prior learning, which occurs independently of faculty supervision — faculty need to have a clear definition of standards against which the evidence of learning is to be judged. As Serling (1980, p. 1) describes it, evaluation is "a comparison between the evidence presented by a student and some reasonable and consistent standard. Well-defined, explicit standards serve as the cornerstone for valid and reliable evaluation." Though specificity about standards is essential for all evaluation, it is especially crucial in assessing experiential learning, where faculty are forced to rely on what Willingham (1977) calls some form of holistic, expert judgment tht is often based on a private process that is not easily communicated or trained.

In order to assure that assessment is equitable from student to student, faculty must state clearly and in sufficient detail the desired learning outcomes for their courses and degree programs. Learners, too, must be assisted in developing specific learning objectives, in the case of sponsored learning, and articulating specific learning outcomes, in the case of both sponsored and prior learning. They must be shown where their experiential learning fits within course and degree requirements. Barton (1976, p. 129) extends this call for clarity and specificity to the overall institution: "Each institution that wants to grant academic credit for experience should state in as precise terms as it can what changes it expects to see in students who have successfully negotiated its processes. Then it will know what to look for in people who have had experience and not instruction. The process would be one of determining what it is students learn through education, and then looking at other individuals to see how much of it they have."

Despite the similar measurement problems facing faculty assessing sponsored and prior experiential learning, faculty see sponsored and prior learning programs as two very different creatures. They are usually administered by separate offices within colleges—sponsored learning by the academic departments themselves or by an internship or career placement office, for example, and prior learning by the continuing education or adult learning office. The practitioners who direct sponsored and prior learning programs belong, for the most part, to different organizations and networks; the two kinds of programs tend to attract and serve very different student clienteles. Even the Council for the Advancement of Experiential Learning, which began in 1974 to improve the assessment of all experiential learning, has developed separate task forces, guidebooks and sourcebooks, and workshops and panels for sponsored and prior learning.

Even more important, the level of acceptance of sponsored experiential learning is much higher than for prior learning. The results of a CAEL survey (Knapp and Davis, 1978) illustrate this point. Sent to 300 CAEL institutions and a representative sample of non-CAEL institutions, the survey was designed to reveal the extent to which sponsored and prior learning programs were in operation in colleges and universities, and to clarify existing policies, procedures, program rationales, and program administration models. It showed that 76.7 percent of the CAEL institutions and 65 percent of the non-CAEL institutions had one or more sponsored learning programs, with 58.7 percent and 45.7 percent, respectively, awarding credit toward degree requirements for sponsored learning. In the case of prior learning programs, however, only 47 percent of the CAEL institutions and 39 percent of the non-CAEL institutions had operational programs and/or procedures for recognizing prior learning.

These percentages are misleading in that even in the institutions with operational programs a very small percentage had programs in which students could prepare portfolios of their prior experiential learning and then undergo individual assessment by faculty experts. Instead, most colleges used College-Level Examination Program (CLEP) tests, other standardized proficiency tests or faculty-made tests; some colleges honored credit recommendations from the American Council of Education (ACE) *Guide to Educational Programs in Noncollegiate Organizations*. In many cases, credit by examination was the only assessment procedure used.

This widespread use of testing for prior learning raises an important distinction: assessing prior experiential learning, such as learning from paid or volunteer work or from homemaking, is different than assessing prior learning that was gained through, for example, a traditional classroom course in an industry or military setting. Learning through the information assimilation mode does lend itself to testing, while experiential learning does not. In analyzing the survey findings, Knapp and Davis concluded that: (1) CAEL institutions are more likely to use additional individualized assessment techniques than other colleges and universities; (2) higher education, as represented by the non-CAEL sample, is more conservative in granting recognition for prior learning and chooses a more standardized approach to assessment; and (3) CAEL institutions are more likely to award more credits per student for prior learning than non-CAEL institutions.

In spite of these important differences between the acceptance of prior learning assessment in CAEL and non-CAEL institutions, however, the fact remains that prior learning programs were less common in all colleges and universities than sponsored learning programs. In my experience, this is still the case, though the number of prior learning programs has grown dramatically during the past four years. Yet the same range of assessment techniques was reportedly used by faculty in evaluating sponsored and prior learning—interviews with learners, performance tests, observations, simulations, examinations, and product assessment. Why is it, then, that assessing prior learning is still viewed as such a radical educational practice, while assessment of sponsored learning appears to be viewed as an integral part of most preprofessional programs and as an enrichment of many liberal arts programs? Is it simply that prior learning assessment is a more recent innovation? As I suggested earlier, the answer seems less related to measurement issues than to political and philosophical issues within the academy.

First, prior learning assessment programs are relative newcomers on the educational scene. In 1974, when the CAEL project began, only a handful of institutions granted credit for prior experiential learning, and most of those that did were nontraditional institutions such as Thomas Edison State College in New Jersey and Empire State College in New York, whose missions were to serve adults. Sponsored experiential learning, on the other hand, has a long tradition within higher education, though it has had many other names. Laboratory sciences, for example, gradually gained acceptance as legitimate college courses during the 1800s, although they too were controversial when they were first proposed at Yale. Clinical experience has been with us since the 1870s, when the medical students at Johns Hopkins first visited hospital wards as a formal part of their training. Cooperative education, in which students alternate periods of on-campus study with periods of off-campus work, has been around for almost seventy years. Practice teaching and other preprofessional practica are required in many prestigious programs, and field study has become a routine option for majors in anthropology, botany, sociology, and related fields. Though the more recent forms of sponsored experiential learning, such as service-learning internships, cross-cultural internships, and career exploration programs, are still struggling to achieve institutionalization within liberal arts curricula, these options are becoming more established as student pressure for career relevance and practicality mounts.

Second, adult learners themselves, for whom prior learning assessment programs were designed, are relative newcomers on the educational scene. Though continuing education and extension programs have been in place in higher education for many years, adults have rarely been seen as an important population to recruit actively. In fact, most institutions have had registration, scheduling, and financial policies that discouraged part-time, older students. The dramatic growth in enrollment of adult students, primarily women, during the past eight years has occurred at the same time that the academy has been faced with the prospect of precipitous drops in enrollment of traditional students, declines that are now a reality in some regions of the country.

Both trends have presented administrators and faculty with a host of new problems and issues. In the eyes of many faculty, therefore, prior learning programs are lumped together with a spate of nontraditional options that colleges are using to attract older students and thereby offset enrollment declines—extension courses, weekend degree programs, adult development workshops, telecourses, and the like. Regardless of the educational merits of granting credit for prior college-level learning, it is easy for faculty to ignore the educational issues and to focus instead on the threat to quality that they believe all adult special programs represent. Understandably but regrettably, in an effort to protect the academic integrity of their institutions, many faculty develop a knee-jerk, critical attitude to all nontraditional programs—and to the nontraditional students they serve. Sponsored experiential learning, in contrast, serves primarily the traditional student and is not as visible a target in most institutions because it is handled in a more decentralized fashion.

Third, and this is one of the most discussed differences between the two, faculty feel that assessing sponsored experiential learning gives them greater control over, and greater participation in, the learning process than they have in prior learning. Sponsored learning, in theory, is an extension of the classroom. It involves faculty in educating students; learning objectives for an internship are, theoretically, mutually established, classroom theory is applied to practice; and learning is evaluated in the context of an ongoing relationship between faculty member, supervisor, and student. Prior learning, on the other hand, is seen as a credentialling process rather than an educational one. The concern is that faculty will simply evaluate disembodied pieces of learning and determine where they fit into the curriculum and that there will be no relationship between student and faculty member.

The reality of sponsored and prior learning programs is, of course, somewhat different than the perception. While some sponsored learning programs are, in fact, structured to foster student-faculty interaction, in many cases faculty do no more than visit the student once or twice during the term, read a letter from the student's supervisor, or evaluate a student's journal after the fact. When a student is placed in another city for an internship, it is often impossible for the faculty member to supervise in any direct way. Frequently, the student's supervisor assumes the role of mentor-teacher and the faculty member becomes a credentialler or verifier of what has been learned.

The same diversity characterizes prior learning programs. While it is true that evaluation based on pre-established learning objectives is not possible in prior learning programs, many programs are structured so that faculty-student interaction is extensive during the portfolio development, educational planning, and assessment processes. In some colleges, faculty teach workshops on portfolio development and degree planning and are intimately involved in helping students articulate their learning. In others, faculty formally assess students only after they have prepared their learning claim with the help of a counselor; in still others, there is no direct faculty-student contact. In programs in which there is more opportunity for faculty-student interaction, faculty often report that, to their surprise, assessment becomes more than a certifying process. In advising the student about the fit between prior learning and degree requirements at the college, in interviewing the student about his or her knowledge of a particular subject, or in assigning the student additional reading to supplement his or her knowledge in a field, faculty become educators and not simply verifiers of learning.

The point here is that in both sponsored and prior learning programs, the most important factor in assuring faculty involvement and control over the learning process is how the program is structured, not whether the student's learning takes place during the term or five years before enrolling in the college or university. Though college-level learning is difficult to define, most faculty have little difficulty in recognizing it when they see it, regardless of the circumstances under which it was gained.

A fourth area of concern with regard to prior experiential learning which differentiates it from sponsored learning in the eyes of educators is that the prior learning does not usually fit easily into existing courses at the college.

In many academic departments, internship, field study, cooperative education, or practicum courses are already in the catalog; students simply sign up for them and regardless of what is actually learned the credits are granted under those established course numbers. In the case of prior learning, each learning claim involves a judgment as to its place in the curriculum. Is a drug and alcohol treatment specialist's learning, for example, equivalent to a general counseling, social work, or human services course? Is Business Management 102 equivalent to a man's learning in business which he gained as an assistant plant engineer for an electronic equipment manufacturing firm? Does the fact that he took an in-house principles of management course guarantee that his learning fits Business Management 102? Which advanced course in business should he now take? Not only is the question of what to call prior learning difficult, but what new learning is most appropriate also needs to be answered. In sponsored learning, the place of the internship or fieldwork in the curriculum has already been established.

As revealed in the Knapp-Davis survey, many colleges approve for credit only prior learning which can be demonstrated through standardized tests such as CLEP exams. If the learner can pass the test, the course can then be entered on the transcript and follow-up courses for the student can be determined. For those colleges attempting to assess experiential learning through individualized assessment techniques, the question of equivalency of the learning is a knotty problem. Some institutions award credit only if the faculty member can certify that the prior learning is equivalent to an established course. Others create special topics courses, course titles to fit the content of the learning, or grant credit in general blocks, such as six credits in introductory social sciences. Whatever approach is taken, this is usually one of the most debated issues when the idea of introducing a prior learning program is introduced.

A fifth cause of resistance to prior learning assessment is that it is rarely factored into faculty workload and full-time equivalent (FTE) generating formulas. Where sponsored learning is offered for credit, it is listed under a course number and therefore generates FTEs. Unfortunately, prior learning assessment is usually viewed as a service or support function as opposed to an instructional activity. Therefore, faculty are frequently paid for assessment on an hourly basis or on the basis of the number of credits the student is requesting. This compensation is rarely adequate. Some administrators even make the mistake of starting prior learning programs with voluntary faculty participation. In some colleges, faculty are expected to do assessment as a regular, uncompensated faculty responsibility — much like academic advising or committee service. In all these examples, since assessment remains outside the credit-generating machinery of the college, there is less incentive for faculty to become involved.

A related problem is that most colleges find that money is lost during the first couple of years of operation of a high quality prior learning program, in which there is adequate counseling and degree planning for adults, reliable assessment procedures, and a trained core of faculty assessors. This means that prior learning program managers face a number of potential financial disincentives: lack of adequate faculty compensation, the tension between administrative concern for cost-effectiveness and academic concern for quality, and the fact that most employers do not have provisions in their tuition aid plans for covering the cost of assessment. Nor can federal and state financial aid funds be used for assessment, even though the cost of assessment is usually one-third to one-fourth the cost of tuition.

Another important difference between sponsored and prior learning programs is that the rationales educators often use for developing them are vastly different. Sponsored learning programs are usually viewed as a way for students to apply theory in a field setting, as a source of financial aid for students, as a way to enrich the curriculum and make it more relevant, as a vehicle for career exploration and personal growth, or as a mechanism for providing community service. The enrollment crunch has caused some colleges to begin using their cooperative education or internship programs as recruiting tools, but for the most part, these programs are still publicized primarily within the already enrolled student body.

In contrast, prior learning programs are used as a way to attract new adult students. Continuing education practitioners are well aware that marketing special options such as assessment of prior learning is essential if their colleges are to offset enrollment declines. This is not to say that there are no educational rationales for introducing assessment; the idea that college-level learning should be recognized regardless of when or where it takes place is the educational rationale most cited by respondents in the Knapp-Davis survey. But the educational rationale is too often ignored in favor of the economic — the case is made that prior learning assessment attracts adults who otherwise would not be in the college. The problem with these economic arguments and the "social justice for the uncredentialled" arguments advanced by experiential learning advocates is that they are the prime targets of faculty who claim to be guardians of academic quality.

The last major difference between sponsored and prior learning has been mentioned briefly elsewhere in this chapter — that the programs serve very different student clienteles through very different administrative arrangements. Continuing education has always been a second-class office on college campuses and adult learners have always been second-class citizens. Now that colleges are increasingly dependent on adult enrollments, and are reluctantly making adjustments in schedules and admissions policies, faculty are being forced to adjust as well. They are coming to see that part-time, older students can learn and can compete effectively with younger students; that they are serious, highly motivated, practical and often more self-directed than younger students; that they have rich experiences to bring to bear on what they are learning, and may have been prompted to return to college by a major life transition or crisis; that they are often extremely insecure about returning to school; and that a majority of them are women. Faculty must, therefore, approach adults somewhat differently than traditional undergraduates.

Sponsored learning, on the other hand, does not require such fundamental changes in attitude and policy. First, it is viewed as serving traditional students who have met regular admissions criteria and who sometimes have been through a rigorous selection process, not adults whom faculty are afraid might have entered through the back door of continuing education. Second, sponsored learning is often so integrated into departmental majors that the faculty criticism which does surface is too dispersed to have much effect. Where one central experiential education office on campus coordinates all sponsored learning, that office is sometimes, like continuing education, singled out for second-class treatment and criticism, but the fact that faculty are used to supervise students in the field and that grades are given help to allay some of the faculty concern.

Having said that these seven issues are most important in the relative acceptance of prior and sponsored experiential learning, and that assessment of learning from life and work experience is similar for the two, I wish to emphasize that all experiential learning programs could be strengthened by encouraging faculty to become more sophisticated in the use of a variety of measurement techniques, to work in assessment teams rather than as isolated experts, to clarify the learning outcomes of their courses and degree programs so that learning claims can be measured against more specific standards, and to become more familiar with experiential learning theory and adult development theory. Training is needed in each of these areas; if faculty who evaluate sponsored and prior learning could be participants in the same workshops, the traning would be even more powerful. In the long run, such training could lead to improved assessment in the classroom and to more widespread support for experiential learning options.

In addition, new measurement techniques and program models need to be devised to save money and faculty time and to preserve individualization so that the educational process in both sponsored and prior learning can be enhanced. For example, group workshops for portfolio development have proven to be more cost-effective than one-to-one counseling sessions, and group debriefing sessions after students complete their internships are increasingly popular with students and faculty. Some programs are experimenting with the use of computer-assisted educational planning and portfolio preparation; others are using student peer advising and mentoring to supplement faculty involvement. Groups of institutions in some urban areas have joined together in consortia for the purpose of handling prior learning assessment through a centralized assessment center. The Compact for Lifelong Educational Opportunities (CLEO) in Philadelphia operates an assessment center for nineteen of its thirty-five member institutions. For each prior learning area to be evaluated, CLEO hires two faculty assessors, one from the college in which the student plans to enroll and one from another similar institution in the region. Rather than pay for an entire in-house assessment program which serves a small number of students, each institution pays an annual membership fee to CLEO. In addition to counseling students in portfolio preparation, CLEO hires faculty experts, organizes the assessment process, creates a transcript-like document for use by college registrars, and conducts periodic faculty training seminars. Similar consortial centers could be established for placement and evaluation of students in sponsored learning experiences; in fact, the idea has already been proposed by several institutions in Philadelphia as a natural outgrowth of current CLEO activities.

Last, new financing models need to be developed that are more supportive of faculty involvement in all experiential learning programs. There are already a few colleges in which assessment of prior learning compensation has become a negotiated item in faculty contracts; some states are considering a faculty workload formula for prior learning assessment. These pioneering efforts should be investigated. Training workshops should be conducted for budget examiners and vice-presidents for finance and administration. Though credit-bearing sponsored learning offered under specific course numbers does generate FTEs, as mentioned above, current financing arrangements do not, at most institutions, take into account the extra faculty travel and time involved in field supervision. When faculty are approached by students to oversee special field projects where there is no official course designation except "independent study," faculty are often not compensated. Investigation of current compensation models would be helpful in sponsored as well as prior learning, with appropriate follow-up training.

In conclusion, several points need to be raised about the contribution experiential learning is making to higher education today. Awarding credit for learning from life and work experience suggests that the workplace, the home, and the community are all potential learning environments where college-level learning can be gained. Experiential learning forces institutions to recognize that they are not the sole providers of postsecondary education and that they must begin to pay attention to the other educational providers in the human learning system—the corporations, the media, labor unions, churches museums and other cultural institutions, and professional organizations. It demonstrates that there is a need for the learner to establish learning goals rather than passively fitting into the structure of the institution. It brings attention to the fact that the financing of higher education needs to be reformed to take into account new faculty roles.

The successes of students who have participated in experiential learning programs imply that our current degree programs should be examined and modified so that all students have the opportunity to learn through both the traditional and experiential modes. In short, experiential learning is gradually bringing about fundamental changes in higher education which will strengthen it and help to maintain its central role in American society.

References

Barton, P. E. "Learning through Work and Education." In M. T. Keeton (Ed.), *Experiential Learning: Rationale, Characteristics, and Assesssment.* San Francisco: Jossey-Bass, 1976.

Coleman, J. S. "Differences Between Experiential and Classroom Learning." In M. T. Keeton (Ed.), *Experiential Learning: Rationale, Characteristics, and Assessment.* San Francisco: Jossey-Bass, 1976.

Council for the Advancement of Experiential Learning. *Faculty Development Program Resource Book.* Columbia, Md.: Council for the Advancement of Experiential Learning, October 1976.

Forrest, A., Knapp, J. E., and Pendergrass, J. "Tools and Methods of Evaluation." In M. T. Keeton (Ed.), *Experiential Learning: Rationale, Characteristics, and Assessment.* San Francisco: Jossey-Bass, 1976.

Keeton, M. T., and Tate, P. J. (Eds.). *Learning by Experience — What, Why, How.* New Directions for Experiential Learning, no. 1. San Francisco: Jossey-Bass, 1978.

Knapp, J., and Davis, L. "Scope and Varieties of Experiential Learning." In M. T. Keeton and P. J. Tate (Eds.), *Learning by Experience — What, Why, How.* New Directions for Experiential Learning, no. 1. San Francisco: Jossey-Bass, 1978.

Serling, A. "The Process of Evaluation." Saratoga Springs, New York: Empire State College, March, 1980.

Willingham, W. *Principles of Good Practice in Assessing Experiential Learning.* Columbia, Md.: Council for the Advancement of Experiential Learning, 1977.

Pamela J. Tate is editor-in-chief of New Directions for Experiential Learning. *Formerly assistant vice chancellor for alternative and continuing education at the State University of New York, she is currently completing a Ph.D. at the Annenberg School of Communications, University of Pennsylvania. She is on the staff of CLEO (Compact for Lifelong Educational Opportunities) in Philadelphia, where she directs a FIPSE-funded project providing life/career planning services for adults in business, industry, and labor.*

Determining the relevance of previously acquired knowledge for
a criterion not associated with the original experience is a
major problem in the assessment of prior incidental learning.

Assessing Prior
Learning Experiences

Ruth B. Ekstrom

As every adult recognizes, much of what is learned in life comes through experience rather than formal education. But problems often arise when we try to convince others that we have acquired knowledge and skills as the result of things we did in the past. Assessing prior learning is a problem both for education and for business. The crux of this problem is determining the congruence between learning that took place at another time and place and the current standards or requirements of the educational institution or employer.

Varieties of Prior Learning

There are many kinds of prior learning. This term applies to any learning that took place in the past but is, only now, being assessed. Some but not all prior learning is experiential in its nature. Prior learning can be categorized in a four-cell matrix (see Figure 1) with the main variables being whether the learning is intentional or incidental and whether it has been supervised and is, therefore, easily verifiable or is difficult to verify. The differences among these four types of prior learning are important clues to the types of measurement needed to assess them.

R. B. Ekstrom (Ed.). *Measurement, Technology, and Individuality in Education.* New Directions for Testing and Measurement, no. 17. San Francisco: Jossey-Bass, March 1983.

Figure 1. A Taxonomy of Learning Experiences

	Intentional	Incidental
Easily Verified	Traditional classroom instruction Most sponsored experiential learning Training programs and courses in business, the military, or voluntary organizations Other noncredit courses	Most learning from paid work Learning from supervised volunteer work
Difficult to Verify	Self-directed study '	Most learning from volunteer work and community service Learning from homemaking Learning from travel, hobbies, TV, reading, and so on Learning from individual development and life experiences

Intentional, easily verified learning includes all traditional classroom instruction. It also includes most sponsored experiential learning. Other types of nonexperiential prior learning also fall in this category — such as instruction offered in noncredit courses sponsored by business and industry, by unions and professional groups, by voluntary organizations and community groups, and by adult education programs. These kinds of prior learning differ from traditional classroom instruction primarily because they are noncredit. The learner is aware of the learning goals and the learning can be verified by the instructor.

Intentional, difficult to verify learning can be equated with self-directed study. This kind of learning is done by people who buy language cassettes, computer courses, and other learning materials for their own use. It is also done by people who plan their own program of reading and study. Self-study differs from traditional education in that the learning goals are usually self-determined rather than externally imposed. In addition, there is no individual, other than the learner, who has supervised or monitored the learning and who can verify what has been learned. The description of the type, scope, and quality of the learning must come from the individual learner.

Incidental learning occurs as a by-product of some other activity. The individual did not set out upon this task with learning as a primary goal. A major problem in assessing incidental learning is that the individual is sometimes not aware that learning has taken place.

Incidental, easily verified learning takes place most frequently in paid work. However, it also occurs as a part of some kinds of unpaid work, such as supervised volunteer work. Although the individual acquires new skills and knowledge as a result of doing work, accomplishing the work itself, rather than teaching the worker, is the primary goal. However, because the work is supervised and often evaluated, it becomes possible to verify and obtain independent evaluation of the scope of the experience and the quality of the work performed.

Incidental, hard-to-verify learning occurs in conjunction with unpaid work, such as homemaking or unsupervised volunteer work and community service. It also includes learning that results from participation in travel and hobbies or from reading or watching television. Finally, incidental, hard-to-verify learning occurs in conjunction with living and developmental experiences. Anyone who has muttered "well, I'm older but wiser" has recognized this type of learning. More often, however, people do not realize that they are learning as they progress through life's experiences. Without the guidance of a teacher or supervisor it is difficult to recognize that intellectual growth has occurred.

Given these widely different varieties of prior learning, how can colleges and employers determine what has been learned, and even more important, whether the learning is relevant for a particular educational program or occupation?

Measurement Problems in Assessing Prior Learning

There has been considerable debate about the need for special techniques for assessing prior experience learning. The focus of this debate is whether it is possible to equate all types of experiential learning, both concurrent sponsored learning and prior learning, or whether assessing prior learning presents assessment problems which differ from those in concurrent learning. The assessment of prior learning, whether experiential or traditional, usually requires techniques that are not necessary for supervised experiential or traditional learning.

Assessment of prior learning requires measurement innovation. There are four basic instruments or measurement techniques needed to assess prior learning: (1) instruments that identify an individual's learning experiences or opportunities to learn; (2) instruments that map the breadth and depth of the learning that occurred in these experiences; (3) techniques that show how an individual's learning relates to existing educational or occupational standards and requirements; and (4) instruments that allow individuals to demonstrate the quality of their prior learning in relation to these standards.

Current Methods of Assessing Prior Learning

The three approaches to assessing prior learning commonly used by colleges are: (1) tests, (2) credit recommendations, and (3) individualized assessment.

According to a survey of 211 colleges which grant academic recognition for nonsponsored learning (Knapp and Davis, 1978), tests are the most widely used of these three methods. As shown in Table 1, the College-Level Examination Program, a standardized test, is the most widely used method of assessing prior learning. Other popular methods, used by more than half of the colleges surveyed, are faculty made (nonstandardized) tests, credit recommendations for experience in the armed services, portfolio assessment, and credit recommendations for training programs in businesses or other organizations.

Tests, whether standardized or teacher-made, are best suited for assessing intentional prior learning, whether from traditional courses, noncredit courses or training programs, or self-directed study. In these situations, the learner has understood the goals of the learning experience. Similarly, in sponsored experiential learning programs the supervising faculty member identifies the intended learning outcomes from the placement experiences and determines if learning has occurred.

Credit recommendations, like tests, are limited in their usefulness. They are intended to equate the content and level of instruction in training programs and noncredit courses offered in businesses, the military, or other organizations with courses offered by colleges and universities. The recommendations are developed by a team of educators who are knowledgeable

Table 1. Percentage of Colleges Using Various Procedures for Granting Academic Recognition for Prior Learning (n = 211)

Tests

College-Level Examination Program	96.2%
College Proficiency Examination Program	32.8%
Other standardized tests	31.8%
Faculty-made (nonstandardized) tests	81.5%

Credit Recommendations

For experiences in the armed services	70.1%
For noncollegiate courses and training programs	51.2%

Individualized

Portfolio assessment	6.7%
Other techniques	25.6%

Source: Adapted from Knapp and Davis, 1978.

about the subject area. The team examines the content of the program or course and the standards that must be met to complete the course successfully. They then decide if the content and standards are equivalent to what is required by colleges. If the course is deemed to be equivalent, the team makes a recommendation about the number of college credits that should be awarded to individuals who complete the course.

Recommendations are available for military courses (American Council on Education, 1978) and for training offered in business, industry, government, and voluntary organizations (American Council on Education, 1980; University of the State of New York, 1977). When an individual who has taken a training program that has been reviewed wishes to receive college credit for this type of prior learning, it is a simple matter for the college to look up the course, verify that the individual did complete it successfully, and record the appropriate credit equivalents on the transcript. The major advantage of credit recommendations is the speed and ease with which evaluation of this type of prior learning can be done. The most serious drawback of this method is that, because the course rather than the individual has been evaluated, it is impossible to differentiate between individuals whose learning has been outstanding and those who just "squeaked through."

The inherent problems in both tests and credit recommendations have led many individuals to search for more flexible, individualized assessment techniques that are appropriate for evaluating incidental as well as intentional learning. Although many different kinds of individualized assessment, such as demonstrations and simulations, have been used, portfolios have emerged as the most prominent individualized technique. Guides for the development of and evaluation of portfolios have been published by the Council for the Advancement of Experiential Learning (1975). Students are often assisted by an instructor or mentor in preparing their portfolio. Evaluation of the portfolio is typically done by a team of three to five faculty members. The major disadvantage of the portfolio technique is the lack of benchmarks or common metrics. Standards vary widely from college to college and even from department to department within the same college. This has led to concerns about the quality of the learning that is being accredited. It has also led to problems in transferring prior learning credits or in having them accepted by graduate and professional schools (Knapp, 1979).

Assessing Adult Women's Prior Learning

The inadequacies of existing measurement techniques become glaringly apparent when attempting to assess adult women's prior learning. Many colleges and universities have been willing to accept prior experience learning acquired through paid work but unwilling, often because of sex stereotypes, to award academic credit for women's learning from their unpaid work in the home, voluntary organizations, and community groups.

The lack of information about women's unpaid work contributes to the problem. Studies of homemaking have focused on the amount of time spent doing various household tasks or have sought to determine the value of home-making by calculating what it would cost to have these tasks performed by paid workers. Studies of volunteer work have dealt chiefly with the proportion of the population providing different kinds of service. Very few studies address the knowledge, skills, and abilities necessary to do this unpaid work—what women learn from instructing volunteers, the self-directed study evolving from the challenges of unpaid work, or the incidental learning acquired by doing unpaid work.

Therefore, my colleagues and I sought to determine what adult women did as unpaid work and what kind of learning was associated with these experiences. In one survey (Ekstrom, Beier, Davis, and Gruenberg, 1981), we found that adult women were most frequently involved in activities that required verbal or interpersonal skills. Another survey (Ekstrom, 1982) found that women's most common homemaking activities were food preparation and child care and that the most common volunteer work experiences involved administrative work, clerical tasks, communications, and problem solving.

Next we developed methods to help map the skills and knowledge women had acquired from unpaid work experience. To do this we prepared competency statements called the "I Can" lists. The first set of lists relating to volunteer work was developed in cooperation with the Council of National Organizations for Adult Education and appear in the book, *How to Get College Credit for What You Have Learned as a Homemaker and Volunteer* (Ekstrom, Harris, and Lockheed, 1977). More recent work done by Educational Testing Service for Project HAVE Skills has resulted in 27 separate "I Can" lists for a variety of homemaking and volunteer work areas.

The "I Can" lists are an aid for identifying the skills women acquire through unpaid work and other prior learning. They are often used in preparing competency statements for inclusion in portfolios for college credit or in resumes for paid employment. One research study (Neely and Schuley, 1980) had eight women educators who were seeking administrative positions use selected "I Can" lists to develop portfolios showing the relevance of their un-paid work experience. These portfolios were evaluated by twenty-four admin-istrators. The study concluded that portfolios of this type are a valid and reli-able way of presenting skills that employers might otherwise overlook.

Helping women identify and present their unpaid work skills is not suf-ficient, however. It is also important to find out if employers and educators think these skills are relevant and useful in other areas. Consequently, we undertook a study of personnel administrators' perceptions of the job relevance of women's unpaid work. Using 524 items selected from the "I Can" lists by a panel of judges, we developed two questionnaires, one for adult women and one for personnel specialists. The women indicated the extent of their experience in each of these skill areas. The personnel specialists rated these same skills twice, first to indicate the extent to which they felt the skill could be transferred to paid jobs and second to indicate the kind of paid jobs most likely to require each skill. We used the findings from this study to develop the HAVE Skills Chart. This is intended as a guidance tool to help women, counselors, and employers see the relationship between women's unpaid work experience and paid jobs. We also used this information to develop the HAVE Skills Survey, a self-report instrument that can be used by employment counselors and personnel offices to screen adult women who are reentering the labor force and to identify those who indicate that they have job-relevant skills for selected occupational areas.

The results of this study (Ekstrom, 1982) show that, while the overall correlation between the extent of women's experience in unpaid work and the perceived job relevance of that experience is low (.15), there are higher and significant relationships in many experience areas. In twelve areas of unpaid work we found a significant relationship between the extent of women's experience and the perceived job relevance of that experience. This suggests that adult women with unpaid work experience and skills in office and clerical work, administration and management, communications and public relations, problem solving, financial management and sales, or counseling and interpersonal skills will have relatively little difficulty transfering this experience to the paid work force. Skills that were related primarily to homemaking were, in general, seen as less job relevant that those that were related to other types of unpaid work.

The HAVE Skills materials do not, however, answer the most difficult question in assessing women's prior learning. That is: "Is this individual's prior experience learning relevant for this specific job or for this particular educational program?" We tried to deal with this question in Project ACCESS (Ekstrom, 1981). First we drew up lists of the functional, work-specific, and self-management skills needed in the ten occupations and the ten areas of vocational education that were the focus of the study. Next we asked small samples of employers to rate these skills as to their importance in selecting new workers. Vocational educators were asked to make the ratings based on the usefulness of the skills in determining course exemption or advanced placement in the program. The most important skills for each occupation and program were then compiled into new scales which are part of an instrument called the Experience Description Summary.

This self-report instrument was then used as part of a counseling program for 155 women who were considering a return to the labor force. Six months later we contacted the employers of the forty-nine women who had obtained paid jobs. The employers made a global evaluation of the women's job performance and also rated them on the skills that were included in the Experience Description Summary. The global ratings showed that 69 percent of these women were considered above average employees and that none was considered to be a below average employee. The women tended, in general, to undervalue their own skills in comparison with their employers' ratings. While significant correlations were obtained between several of the occupational scales and the employer ratings, the sample size in this study was too small (because of deteriorating labor market opportunities) for any meaningful differential validity study of these scales.

Other Innovations in Assessing Prior Learning

Other techniques have also been developed to help colleges and employers evaluate prior learning in a flexible, individualized manner but with some type of standardized criteria. Both the benchmarks approach to scoring work experience narratives and self-report instruments that relate experience to the standards of a specific program or occupation are promising solutions to this problem.

The benchmark approach is used by the federal government's Office of Personnel Management. It consists of a three-step job analysis and evaluation procedure. Subject matter experts first identify the knowledge, abilities, skills, and other characteristics (KASOs) required in the job and then select those they feel best differentiate between superior employees and marginal employees. Next the subject matter experts read a number of work experience descriptions. These are then rated for their relevance to the KASOs. The narratives on which there is the greatest agreement (that is, they have the smallest standard deviations) are selected as benchmarks. These benchmarks are then used operationally to score the experience narratives of actual job applicants. The experience narrative format requires job applicants to describe their major accomplishments in a specific area, such as the ability to do financial analysis. The subjects are asked to identify the problem or objective in a relevant situation, to describe what they did and when, to describe the outcome or results and the extent to which the outcome is a result of their personal effort. If education or training is involved, applicants report any grades or evaluations received. Applicants are also asked to give the name of someone who can verify the information. Benchmarks have been developed for unpaid volunteer work (Birch and Davis Associates, 1981) as well as for paid work.

The benchmark approach has not been used by educational institutions. It has several advantages. The benchmarks provide a form of common metric which is not part of the current portfolio evaluation process. When individuals are told the KASOs that are considered relevant, the narratives can be much more specific than is typically the case in portfolios.

Assessing prior experience learning through self-report measures also holds high promise for the future. As indicated in the Project ACCESS research, work begins with determining what types of experiences are most relevant for the goal of the measurement effort. This technique has been used to evaluate the prior experience of applicants to graduate schools of management (Thornton and Rosenfeld, 1981). The Work Experience Inventory, developed by Thornton and Rosenfeld, provides information both about the level and dimensions of prior paid or unpaid work experiences involving management activities.

All of these methods are beginning attempts at the development of appropriate methodologies for the assessment of prior learning. Hopefully, the growing awareness of the importance of prior experience will bring measurement specialists to develop better techniques and, also, to consider prior experience more carefully when assessing formal learning. In the past, we have too frequently disregarded the relationship between individual experience and test scores. We have tended to assume that all people arrive at a test with the same experience and we all too often bury the evidence of how individual differences in opportunity and motivation to learn affect test scores. The work that has been done in measuring learning from prior experience can be an important tool to help us improve our understanding of the factors affecting scores on traditional tests as well as a tool for understanding more about kinds of learning that we have never before tried to measure.

References

American Council on Education. *A Guide to the Evaluation of Educational Experiences in the Armed Services.* Washington, D. C.: American Council on Education, 1978.

American Council on Education. *The National Guide to Educational Credits for Training Programs.* Washington, D. C.: American Council on Education, 1980.

Birch and Davis Associates. *Development of Unpaid Experience Benchmarks to Be Used in Unassembled Examining.* Silver Spring, Md.: Birch and Davis Associates, 1981.

Council for the Advancement of Experiential Learning. *A Guide for Assessing Prior Experience Through Portfolios.* Columbia, Md.: Council for the Advancement of Experiential Learning, 1975.

Ekstrom, R. B. *Credentialing Women's Life Experience* (Project ACCESS Final Technical Report). Princeton, N.J.: Educational Testing Service, 1981.

Ekstrom, R. B. "Measuring Adult Women's Job-Relevant Life Experience Learning." Paper presented at the annual meeting of the American Psychological Association, Washington, D.C., August 1982.

Ekstrom, R. B., Beier, J., Davis, L., and Gruenberg, B. "The Career and Educational Counseling Implications of Women's Life Experience Learning." *The Personnel and Guidance Journal,* 1981, *60* (2), 97–101.

78

Ekstrom, R. B., Harris, A. M., and Lockheed, M. L. *How to Get College Credit for What You Have Learned as a Homemaker and Volunteer.* Princeton, N.J.: Educational Testing Service, 1977.

Knapp, J. "Do Graduate Schools Discount Experiential Credits?" In S. V. Martorana and E. Kuhns (Eds.), *Transferring Experiential Credit,* New Directions for Experiential Learning, no. 4. San Francisco: Jossey-Bass, 1979.

Knapp, J., and Davis, L. "Scope and Varieties of Experiential Learning." In M. T. Keeton and P. J. Tate (Eds.), *Learning by Experience — What, Why, How.* New Directions for Experiential Learning, no. 1. San Francisco: Jossey-Bass, 1978.

Neely, M. A., and Schuley, M. R. "Turning Experience into Competency Statements." *The Personnel and Guidance Journal,* 1980, *58* (10), 663–665.

Thornton, R. F., and Rosenfeld, M. *Development of a Procedure for Evaluating the Managerial Work Experience of Applicants to Graduate Schools of Management.* (GMAC Research Report 81-6). Princeton, N.J.: Educational Testing Service, 1981.

University of the State of New York. *A Guide to Educational Programs in Noncollegiate Organizations.* Albany: University of the State of New York, 1977.

Ruth B. Ekstrom is a senior research scientist at Educational Testing Service. Her recent work has focused on the assessment of experiential learning and on women's educational and career development.

Index